Buying the Top

How to Spot the Peak Before You Buy In—and Protect Your Money, Career, and Judgment

Simon Blackwood

First edition, 2026

Published by Simon Blackwood

Contents

Foreword

I did not set out to write a book about memory. I set out, a few years ago, to understand a single, narrow, professionally embarrassing fact: a mutual fund I had recommended to a family member, based substantially on a single outstanding year, spent the following three years quietly reverting to a baseline I could have found in about four minutes if I had looked at the right ten-year chart instead of the one-year headline someone had put in front of me. Nobody misled me. The number was real. I simply weighted it the way most people weight the most recent thing they've seen: as though it were the whole story rather than the loudest chapter in a much longer and less dramatic one.

That mistake is not interesting on its own. What became interesting, over the research that followed, was how often the identical mechanism showed up in places that had nothing to do with investing — a manager's memory of an employee's year, a jury's memory of a trial's last witness, a front office's memory of a player's best season, a scientific field's own citation habits. Different stakes, different institutions, the same structural failure: a full, relevant history existing somewhere, and a judgment collapsing instead onto whatever happened most recently, because recent evidence is simply easier to retrieve than older evidence of equal or greater importance.

This book exists because that pattern, once seen, does not un-see itself, and because the correction for it turns out to be more specific and more learnable than "try to remember better." Memory is not going to stop favoring the recent; nothing in this book asks it to. What can change is whether a judgment is allowed to rest on memory alone, unaudited, at the exact moment the freshest evidence is also the most persuasive.

I have no personal stake in whether any particular reader chases the next hot fund, favors the last witness, or overpays for a career year. I have a stake, as anyone does who has made this mistake once and watched it cost something, in the plain fact that the last data point is never nothing — and never, by itself, the whole story either.

Introduction

The last data point doesn't predict the future—it marks the end of the past. Yet investors buy stocks at their peak, committees promote based on recent work, and juries decide based on closing arguments, all because what just happened feels like what happens next. This book is about the most expensive cognitive error you'll make: mistaking the end of a trend for evidence of its continuation.

The moment you're most certain is the moment you should be least certain—because that certainty is built on the last thing you saw, not the full history of what happened before. This book is about a specific failure mode in human judgment: the final data point doesn't just outweigh the rest, it becomes the only one we can actually see. And we act on it with greatest conviction exactly when we're most wrong.

Every January for fifteen years, Bill Miller beat the market. Then the sixteenth year, he didn't. The investors who'd followed his streak and finally opened accounts in 2006—they bought the top. They arrived exactly when the pattern broke, poured in capital at the point of maximum extension, and extrapolated from a terminal value. This book argues that we all do that, not just in financial markets but across every domain where evidence accumulates over time. We systematically mistake endpoints for trends, treating the most recent data point not as one more piece of information but as a verdict that rewrites everything that came before. By the time we realize the pattern was exhausted, we've already committed.

This book examines one cognitive bias — recency bias, the tendency to weight the most recently available evidence more heavily than its actual relevance justifies — across seven domains where the mistake is well documented and the stakes are real: investing, workplace performance review, courtroom testimony, professional sports contracts, economic forecasting, political judgment, personal relationships and memory, and the citation practices of science itself.

Each of the eight domain chapters that follow (Chapters 1 through 8) follows a consistent shape. It opens with a documented pattern or a well-established piece of research, works through the mechanism that produces it, and closes with a composite case — an invented but representative scenario, always explicitly flagged as invented, built to make the abstract mechanism concrete without claiming to describe any specific real person, trial, or institution. Every one of these composite cases is clearly marked as such at the point it's introduced, though the wording of that disclosure varies chapter to chapter; none of them should be read as a documented account of an actual investor, employee, juror, executive, or couple.

The book uses the mutual-fund case in Chapter 1 as its reference point throughout, not because investing is the most important domain it covers, but because it is the one domain where the distortion can actually be measured — fund flows, rankings, and subsequent performance are all trackable in a way a manager's shifting memory of an employee's year is not. Later chapters return to that reference point deliberately, drawing the same mechanism out in domains where the evidence is real but harder to quantify.

Chapter 9 steps back from the domain-by-domain survey and collects four structural techniques — the full-window checklist, contemporaneous documentation, the pre-registered decision criterion, and the assigned longer-horizon role — that recur, in different costumes, across every chapter that precedes it. Readers looking for the practical takeaway without the full domain-by-domain argument can reasonably start there, though the techniques will mean more, and stick better, read after the cases that motivate them.

Each chapter closes with a short, direct turn addressed to the reader — a practical translation of that chapter's argument into a question worth asking the next time recent evidence is doing more work in a judgment than it has actually earned. That turn is the book's real spine; the domains are simply where it gets tested.

Chapter 1: The Last Data Point

Bill Miller's streak ended on the last trading day of December 2005, though nobody knew it yet. For fifteen consecutive years—1991 through 2005—his Legg Mason Value Trust had beaten the S&P; 500 every single calendar year. Not almost every year. Not most years. Every year, without exception, for longer than most marriages last.

For fifteen consecutive years—1991 through 2005—his Legg Mason Value Trust had beaten the S&P; 500 every single calendar year. Not almost every year. Not most years. Every year, without exception, for longer than most marriages last. By late 2005, *Barron's* had run out of superlatives and settled on calling him "the greatest money manager of our time," which is the kind of thing financial journalists write when they need to fill column inches before the New Year's deadline and can't think of anything that won't sound hyperbolic six months later.

Money poured in. At the peak in 2006, the fund held over $20 billion in assets—up from about $700 million when the streak started in 1991.

Most of that $20 billion arrived in the final three years.

Think about that timing. Fifteen years of exceptional performance, but the bulk of the investor capital showed up only after year twelve. Only after the story had been told and retold so many times it stopped sounding like news and started sounding like established fact. Like something you'd be foolish *not* to know about.

I want you to picture one of those investors. Call her Sarah—though I've met a dozen Sarahs over the years, and if you work anywhere near finance or just pay attention to your retirement account, you probably have too.

Early forties. Marketing director at a midsized firm in Charlotte, North Carolina. Saves diligently—always has, even back when she was making $32,000 a year and putting away fifty bucks a paycheck felt heroic. Checks her retirement account maybe once a quarter unless something scares her, at which point she checks it obsessively for three days straight and then doesn't look again for two months. She's read *The Total Money Makeover* cover to cover, highlighted passages, lent it to her sister. She's watched enough Suze Orman to know the basics: diversify, minimize fees, don't panic-sell when the market drops, automate your savings so you never see the money in the first place.

She's not financially illiterate. She's not reckless. She's not the person who shows up in cautionary tales about day-trading their mortgage payment on penny stocks they found on Reddit.

One morning in January 2006, she's scrolling her phone over coffee—still in her robe, hair wet from the shower, toast burning slightly in the toaster because she got distracted, that narrow window before her nine-year-old daughter wakes up when the house is actually quiet—and sees a year-end fund performance table someone posted in a personal finance forum she follows. Bill Miller's name sits at the top. Fifteen years listed next to it in bold.

She screenshots the article.

She doesn't do anything with it immediately. She's busy. Her daughter has a science fair project due Friday and hasn't started it. There's a product launch at work that's eating up sixty-hour weeks.

The dog needs to go to the vet. Life happens, and it's not like she makes financial decisions based on headlines she scrolls past while drinking coffee and trying to remember if she paid the water bill.

But the number stays with her.

Fifteen years. Longer than her daughter has been alive. Longer than she's been at her current job. Longer than she's lived in this house, longer than she's been married—though she doesn't think about that last one too hard because the marriage ended two years ago and she's still sorting out what financial independence actually looks like when you're doing it alone in your forties with a kid and a mortgage.

A week later she's reviewing her 401(k) allocations at her desk during lunch, eating a sad salad out of a plastic container with one hand and clicking through her account with the other, trying not to get vinaigrette on her keyboard. Most of her money is in index funds, like it's supposed to be. Vanguard. Fidelity. The boring stuff. The stuff that compounds slowly and never makes you feel smart but also never makes you feel stupid, which is most of what investing is supposed to be if you're not trying to beat the market for a living.

But she's been reading articles—lots of them, lately, because she's responsible for her own retirement now and that feels different than when there were two incomes—about how index funds just give you average returns. Market returns. Which is fine, except she's forty-two and her retirement account balance is lower than it should be because of the divorce settlement and because she took time off when her daughter was born and because she spent her twenties paying off student loans instead of investing. Average might not be enough. She needs better than average. She needs to catch up.

And here's a guy who's beaten average for fifteen straight years.

She pulls up the fund's page. Reads the manager bio. Reads the investment philosophy—something about value investing, buying what's out of favor, being willing to look wrong in the short term to be right in the long term. It sounds careful. Deliberate. Not reckless. Not like gambling. Like a disciplined strategy executed by someone who actually knows what they're doing.

She's not talking about going all-in. That would be crazy, and she knows it. Just reallocating a slice. Maybe 20 percent. She's still keeping her index funds. She's still diversified. She's still being responsible.

She logs in and moves $80,000 into Legg Mason Value Trust.

It doesn't feel reckless. It feels measured, informed, even a little bit shrewd—like she's found something most people haven't noticed yet, or like she's finally taking control instead of just letting her money sit there on autopilot. Like she's being strategic. Like she's doing what smart investors do: looking at the evidence and making an active choice based on what's clearly working.

Except, of course, that billions of dollars of other people's money had the same idea, which is how the fund got to $20 billion in the first place.

The secret everybody knew.

In 2007, the fund dropped 6.7 percent while the S&P; 500 gained 5.5 percent.

The streak was over.

Sarah noticed—the quarterly statement showed up in her mailbox in a thin envelope, and she opened it standing at the kitchen counter, still holding her car keys, daughter already buckled in the car waiting to go to soccer practice—but she didn't panic. One bad year after fifteen good ones? That's noise. Statistical variance. You don't bail after one year. That's exactly the kind of emotional decision she'd been trained not to make, the kind of mistake all those personal finance books warn against in chapters with titles like "Stay the Course" and "Ignore the Noise."

In 2008, Legg Mason Value Trust fell 55 percent.

Fifty-five percent.

Not a typo. Not a reporting error. Fifty-five actual percent of the account value, gone, vaporized in a market collapse that felt, at the time, like it might not have a bottom.

The kind of loss that doesn't just show up as a red number on a statement—it rewires how you sleep. Sarah started checking the balance every morning before work, still in bed with her phone, the blue light harsh in the dark room, daughter still asleep down the hall. She'd lie awake doing the math: if it falls another 20 percent, that's X; if it falls 30 percent, that's Y; if it goes to zero—and there were days in October and November 2008 when zero felt plausible, when the news was talking about bank failures and systemic risk and whether the entire financial system might collapse—that's her daughter's college fund gone. That's retirement pushed back a decade. That's starting over at forty-four with nothing.

By early 2009, her $80,000 had become $38,000.

She sold. Right at the bottom, as it turned out, though she didn't know that at the time. She just knew she couldn't watch it fall further. Couldn't stomach opening her account one more morning and seeing another five percent gone. Couldn't take the insomnia, the constant dread, the feeling of watching her future drain away in real time while she did nothing.

Five years later, in 2014, that $38,000 was still sitting in a money market fund earning effectively nothing—less than 1 percent, barely keeping pace with inflation, certainly not recovering the ground she'd lost. She never put it back into stocks. The memory of watching half her savings evaporate was more vivid, more *real*, more emotionally present than any chart showing the market's recovery or any article explaining that stocks always come back or any rational calculation of what she should do next. The scar tissue was permanent. The intellectual knowledge that she should buy back in, that she was making the mistake worse by staying in cash, couldn't overcome the visceral memory of what losing felt like.

She wasn't alone.

By 2012, the fund had shrunk to less than $3 billion—down from $20 billion at the peak. Most of the money that arrived during the streak's final act left during the collapse, and it left at exactly the wrong time, cementing losses that would've been temporary if people had just held on. The investors who got hurt worst were the ones who'd bought in 2004, 2005, 2006—exactly when the story felt most bulletproof, most validated, most impossible to ignore.

They bought because of what the fund had just done.

They sold because of what it was doing now.

Same reason. Same mechanism. Different direction.

They were chasing the last number they could see.

Here's what gets me, and why I keep coming back to this story even though it's been dissected in business school case studies and investor seminars and cautionary blog posts for fifteen years: Bill Miller himself never claimed the streak made him clairvoyant.

In interviews during the run—and I've gone back and read them, because I wanted to see if he was selling the myth or just trapped inside it—he'd openly acknowledge the role of luck. He'd describe mistakes he'd made, positions that blew up, calls he got completely wrong that just happened to be offset by other calls he got right. He'd point out that calendar-year windows are arbitrary. A streak measured January-to-December would look entirely different if you measured February-to-January, or July-to-June, or any other twelve-month rolling window. Shift the starting line by thirty days and the whole narrative collapses. The whole thing could've been a quirk of where you drew the line, nothing more.

None of it mattered.

The streak was the story. The streak was what got printed, what got repeated, what people remembered when they moved their money. What they forgot—or never weighted properly in the first place—was that fifteen years is a blink in market history. That extraordinary runs end, always, without exception, because that's what "extraordinary" means: unusually far from the average, which means regression to the average is the default expectation unless something structural changed. That the very fame of the streak made it a terrible signal for what would happen next, because fame attracts capital, and capital changes everything about how a fund can operate.

A $700 million fund can take concentrated positions in overlooked small-caps, the kind of stocks that move 50 percent on a good quarter because nobody's paying attention yet. You can build a

10 percent position in a company nobody's heard of and it won't move the price when you buy.

A $20 billion fund has to spread across large-caps just to deploy the money. You can't put 10 percent of $20 billion into a small company—that *is* the company. You'd own it outright, and even if you wanted to, you couldn't sell without tanking the price. So you end up in the same mega-cap stocks every other large fund owns, which means you start looking more and more like the index you're supposed to beat.

The strategy that worked at $700 million is structurally impossible at $20 billion.

Miller knew this. He said as much, multiple times. It didn't matter. The money came anyway.

You might be thinking: okay, but this is just one example. One fund, one manager, one period. How do we know this is a pattern and not just an anecdote about Bill Miller?

Fair question. Let me give you the pattern.

This is recency bias in its purest, most concentrated form—the human tendency to treat the most recent evidence as if it were the whole story, even when older, equally valid evidence sits right there in the same dataset, waiting to be considered.

It's not about intelligence. Sarah wasn't stupid. Many of Miller's investors were financially literate; some of them were professionals, people who managed money for a living or at least understood how markets work. Many had read the disclaimer printed on every fund prospectus in bold print at the top of the first page: *Past performance does not guarantee future results.* Many had lived through similar cycles before with different funds, watched other hot managers flame out, maybe even gotten burned themselves in smaller ways.

The knowledge was there.

What failed was the weighting.

The recent evidence just *felt* more real.

Start with how memory actually works, because this matters and because most people's mental model of memory is wrong in a way that makes recency bias invisible.

Human recall is not a filing cabinet where every piece of information sits on an equal shelf, waiting to be retrieved with equal effort whenever you need it. (I wish it were. I'd have a much easier time remembering where I put my keys.) Retrieval is reconstructive, dynamic, biased toward whatever's easiest to access. Recent memories sit closer to the surface because they haven't degraded yet. They haven't been overwritten by newer information crowding the same neural pathways. They haven't faded the way an unrehearsed memory fades after months or years of disuse, the details washing out like an old photograph left in sunlight—still there, technically, but harder to make out, less vivid, less *present*.

When you try to answer the question "How has this fund performed?" your brain doesn't conduct an impartial survey of all available years, weighing each equally like a judge scoring Olympic gymnastics.

It reports back the easiest-to-find answer.

That's almost always the most recent answer.

And it does this so quickly, so automatically, so far below the threshold of conscious deliberation, that you experience the recent number not as one data point among many but as *the* data point. The thing you know. The thing that feels true.

This retrieval asymmetry isn't a bug in the system. For most of human evolutionary history—the 200,000 years we spent hunting and foraging before we invented agriculture, let alone stock markets—recent information genuinely *was* the most useful information.

If you're trying to decide whether a watering hole is safe, last week's evidence about predators matters more than evidence from six months ago. Conditions change. Threats move. A lion pride that was camped near the watering hole in March might've moved fifty miles away by September. Seasons shift. Water quality changes. What was true half a year ago might be completely irrelevant now.

The recent past is a better guide to the immediate future than the distant past.

The heuristic works. It kept us alive long enough to develop agriculture, written language, antibiotics, and eventually 401(k) plans.

The trouble starts when this same shortcut gets applied to domains where recent data points are *not* more informative—where the passage of time doesn't signal a regime change, doesn't mean conditions fundamentally shifted, doesn't mean old evidence expired.

Where random variation makes recent performance *look* like a regime change even when nothing fundamental has shifted.

A mutual fund's one great year might mean the manager discovered a durable edge, a repeatable insight that'll keep working for the next decade.

Or it might mean the sectors they happened to be overweight had a tailwind that year—tech stocks ripped, they owned tech stocks, end of story.

Or it might mean nothing more than statistical noise. A fair coin landing heads five times in a row, which happens more often than you'd think if you actually flip enough coins.

From inside the moment, using only the data available at the time, those explanations are nearly impossible to tell apart.

Skill looks like luck. Luck looks like skill. Temporary streaks look like permanent edges.

Recency bias is what happens when your brain treats every recent deviation as if it were a genuine signal, a real regime change. The same machinery that correctly catches actual shifts—water quality changing, predator patterns evolving, seasonal food availability moving—fires just as readily on noise that merely *looks* like a regime change for exactly one measurement period.

Financial economists have tracked this pattern for decades, and the research is relentlessly, depressingly consistent.

Mutual funds that post standout returns in a given year attract the largest inflows of new money in the following year. Those inflows peak precisely at the funds sitting at the top of the annual rankings—the ones whose performance was so extreme it made the year-end lists published in *Money* magazine and *The Wall Street Journal* and now, increasingly, in viral Twitter threads and TikTok videos with titles like "This fund returned 47% last year and you've never heard of it."

The money doesn't follow a fund's ten-year average. It doesn't follow risk-adjusted returns. It doesn't follow any measure that would require pausing to think about what the number actually means, to dig into *why* the performance happened or whether the conditions that produced it are likely to repeat.

It follows the spike.

Every single time.

What happens next is also consistent, and this is the part that should make your stomach drop: returns mean-revert.

A fund that sits in the 95th percentile of performance one year will, on average, rank closer to the 50th percentile the next year. Not because the manager suddenly got worse. Not because they changed their strategy or lost their edge or started phoning it in. Not because they got lazy or complacent or stopped caring.

But because extreme outcomes are, by definition, unusual.

And unusual outcomes tend to be followed by outcomes closer to the average.

This isn't market-specific. It's not even finance-specific. It shows up everywhere you measure repeated performance under conditions of uncertainty. Batting averages. Test scores. Recovery times after surgery. Corporate earnings. Restaurant quality after a rave review in the *Times*. Podcast downloads after one episode goes viral. A student who scores in the 99th percentile on the SAT the first time will, on average, score lower the second time—not because they got dumber, but because the first score likely included some amount of luck, and luck doesn't repeat on command.

Extremes regress.

The further a result sits from the mean, the more likely the next result is to sit closer to it, simply because extremes don't sustain themselves without some durable structural reason—and durable structural reasons are rarer than random fluctuations that look like structural reasons for exactly one year.

Let me show you how this plays out in practice, because I want you to *feel* the mechanism working on you, not just understand it intellectually. I want you to notice the pull.

It's January. You're flipping through a personal finance magazine—or more likely, scrolling an article someone shared in a Slack channel at work, the kind of passive reading you do while waiting for a meeting to start or standing in line at the grocery store or sitting in the parking lot outside your kid's piano lesson with ten minutes to kill.

It's one of those year-end roundups: "Top Performing Funds of 2023."

One name catches your eye. The fund returned 47 percent last year while the market returned 11 percent.

You pause.

That's not a small gap. That's not noise. That's not the kind of difference that could be explained by fees or luck or measurement error. That's the kind of outperformance that means someone either got very lucky or knows something most managers don't.

You click through to the fund's page.

The five-year average? Mediocre. Mid-single-digit returns, nothing worth mentioning, the kind of performance that wouldn't make any year-end list. But last year was extraordinary. The article includes a Q&A; with the manager, a woman who ran a small hedge fund before launching the mutual fund five years ago. She explains the strategy: focus on undervalued small-caps in specific sectors, hold through volatility, take concentrated positions when conviction is high. She describes her research process—on-site visits to company headquarters, channel checks with suppliers and customers, industry contacts built up over twenty years. She walks through the three or four bets that paid off big last year: early positions in companies that tripled or quadrupled after acquisitions or product launches, moves that in hindsight look brilliant but at the time looked contrarian, even reckless.

It all sounds plausible. Careful. Rigorous. Not like gambling, like *research*.

You screenshot the fund name.

You don't do anything immediately—you're not impulsive, and you know better than to make financial decisions based on one article.

But a week later you're reviewing your retirement account, and there's that fund name again, still in your photos, still sitting there like an unanswered question. You think: I'm not going to go all-in. I'm not abandoning my index funds. Those are staying put. But allocating 15 percent toward something that's clearly working? That's not reckless. That's prudent. That's the kind of active choice that distinguishes someone who pays attention from someone who just lets their money sit on autopilot and hopes for the best.

You make the move.

Two years later, the fund has returned to its historical range. Mid-single-digits, maybe slightly below average after fees. You haven't *lost* money—that's something. But you also haven't gained any ground relative to the broad market index you already owned. The 15 percent you moved has underperformed the 85 percent you left alone, which means your overall return is now lower than it would've been if you'd done nothing.

What you did, without realizing it, was buy a mediocre fund at the exact moment its short-term performance made it look exceptional. You paid an entry price—whether in terms of fees, or concentration risk, or just opportunity cost—calibrated to a return that had already happened and wasn't going to repeat.

Nothing about your decision was unreasoned. You looked at real data. You read the manager's explanation. You considered the track record. You didn't bet the farm—you diversified, kept your index funds, stayed disciplined.

The distortion sits one layer deeper.

It's in *which* part of the track record registered as the operative fact.

A five-year history is five roughly equal-sized pieces of evidence about how a fund performs under different market conditions. Your brain did not treat them equally. It treated the most recent year as the story and the other four as background noise, historical context, something that happened before the manager "figured it out" or "hit their stride" or whatever narrative you unconsciously constructed to make the recent year feel predictive rather than random.

Not because you consciously decided recency mattered more.

But because the recent year was easier to retrieve, more vivid, more emotionally salient, more *there* in your mind at the moment you were making the decision.

That asymmetry shows up everywhere. And—here's the kicker—it shows up regardless of expertise.

Professional analysts fall for it too. Sometimes harder than retail investors, because proximity to the market means constant exposure to new data, which just gives recency bias more fuel.

Samuel Hartzmark, a finance professor at the University of Chicago, published a study looking at how analysts adjust their earnings forecasts in response to recent news. He found that analysts systematically overweight the most recent earnings report relative to the longer trend, even when the recent report is a clear outlier, even when you can see from the five-year history that the company's earnings bounce around a stable range and last quarter was just the high end of that range, not a new regime.

The longer an analyst has covered a stock, the more historical data they've accumulated about its typical performance range.

And yet the most recent quarter still dominates their forecast.

Experience didn't fix it. Expertise didn't remove the bias. It just dressed it up in better credentials and more sophisticated-sounding language.

The same pattern appears in how individual investors trade stocks. Ask someone why they bought a particular stock, and the answer almost always references something that happened recently. A strong earnings beat last quarter. A product launch two weeks ago. A new contract announced last Monday. An analyst upgrade yesterday. A tweet from the CEO this morning that hinted at something big coming.

Rarely—almost never—does anyone say, "I noticed this stock has traded in a consistent range for the past decade, and right now it's near the bottom of that range, so I'm buying with the expectation it'll revert to the mean."

The recent event is what made the stock feel relevant. What triggered the awareness. What your brain filed under "things I know about this company right now." Older data—even older data that's more representative of the company's typical performance, more statistically reliable, more predictive if you actually bothered to weight it properly—gets classified as history, not as forecast material. Background, not signal.

This creates a systematic timing problem that's almost mathematical in its predictability: the moment a stock or a fund or an asset looks most exciting, most worth buying, most like it's "clearly working," is very often the moment right after an extreme positive result.

Which, by the logic of mean reversion, is also the moment right *before* performance is likeliest to disappoint.

Buying what's hot is buying what just peaked.

You're not wrong about what happened. You're just late.

Consider Ken Heebner's CGM Focus Fund, because this one is almost too perfect to believe and yet it happened exactly as I'm about to describe it.

In the decade ending in 2009—so, 2000 through 2009—it was the best-performing mutual fund in America.

Not one of the best. *The* best.

It returned an annualized 18 percent while the S&P; 500 basically went nowhere over the same period, maybe even lost a bit depending on exactly when you measure. Morningstar gave Heebner an award: "domestic stock fund manager of the decade."

Think about that title for a second. Manager of the *decade*. Not manager of the year—manager of ten full years. They gave him a plaque. Wrote a profile. Money flooded in. The fund's assets peaked at nearly $10 billion.

Then, over the next decade—2010 through 2020—the fund underperformed the S&P; 500 by an average of about 13 percentage points per year.

Thirteen percentage points per year. Compounded over a decade.

That's not a rounding error. That's not a bad year or two. That's the difference between wealth and frustration, between retiring on schedule and working another five years, between sending your kid to the college they got into and sending them to the one you can afford.

It wasn't a scandal. Heebner didn't change his strategy. He didn't commit fraud, didn't get caught insider trading, didn't flee to the Cayman Islands with a suitcase full of bearer bonds. The decade that made him famous was, in hindsight, a run of well-timed sector bets during an era when aggressive concentration happened to pay off. Energy stocks ripped, he owned energy. Financials collapsed, he got out early. Housing boomed, he rode it up and sold before it crashed. The following decade punished the same approach—aggressive sector rotation, high turnover, concentrated bets. Same strategy, different market environment, completely different result.

Investors who bought in at the peak—drawn by the "manager of the decade" headline, by the Morningstar award, by the year-end lists and the magazine profiles—experienced the second decade, not the first.

Their timing was set entirely by when the story reached them. When it became famous enough to penetrate their awareness. When the evidence looked overwhelming.

When it felt safest.

I've seen this happen in real time more times than I can count.

Not just with mutual funds—with everything. Cryptocurrencies that 10x'd in a year and then collapsed. Stocks that quintupled and then gave it all back. Real estate markets that felt like they'd never stop rising until they did. Venture-backed startups that looked like sure bets until they weren't.

The pattern never changes. Only the names.

What gets me—and I mean this genuinely bothers me, keeps me up some nights when I think about how many people get hurt by this—is how *reasonable* it all feels in the moment.

You're not being reckless. You're looking at evidence. You're seeing a clear pattern. Fifteen years isn't a fluke—that's longer than most economic cycles. That's long enough to include multiple recessions, multiple bull markets, multiple different market environments. If someone can beat the market for fifteen years straight, that's not luck. That's skill. That's an edge. That's exactly the kind of thing you *should* be paying attention to.

Except it's not skill. Or it's not *just* skill. It's skill plus environment plus timing plus a dozen other factors, many of them random, that happened to align for a period of time and then stopped aligning.

And the evidence that would tell you that—the evidence that would help you distinguish a durable edge from a temporary alignment—is sitting right there in the same dataset. It's the *other* fourteen years. The years before the streak, if there are any. The years after, once enough time has passed. The performance of other managers using similar strategies. The historical base rate of how often streaks like this sustain versus how often they collapse.

But that evidence is older. Harder to retrieve. Less vivid. Less emotionally salient.

It doesn't *feel* as real.

Here's what you can do about this, starting tomorrow morning. Or tonight, if you want. Or right now, if you're the kind of person who reads a chapter and then immediately opens your brokerage account to see if you're making the mistake the chapter just described. (I've done that. More than once.)

Open your investment accounts. All of them—retirement, taxable, 529s for your kids if you have those. Look at what you own.

Now ask yourself: When did I buy this?

Not just the date—though the date matters, and if you can't remember it you should look it up. But more specifically: *What had just happened* when I bought this? What recent performance did I see? What news had just come out? What story was I telling myself about why this was a good investment *right now*?

If the honest answer is "I bought it because it just had a great year" or "I bought it because everyone was talking about it" or "I bought it because it was at an all-time high and I didn't want to miss out," you might be holding the last data point.

You might've bought at the peak.

That doesn't automatically mean you should sell—selling is its own decision with its own set of biases, and panic-selling at the bottom is just recency bias in reverse. But it does mean you should ask the harder question: If this investment *didn't* just have a great year, if I were looking at it with five years of mediocre performance instead of one year of exceptional performance, would I still want to own it?

If the answer is no—if the only reason you own it is because of what it just did—then you're not investing based on what it is.

You're investing based on where it's been.

And where it's been is the one place it's not going back to.

The last data point is always the most seductive. It's the one you can see clearly, the one that feels real, the one that sits right there at the edge of the chart demanding your attention.

It's also the one that's already over.

The question isn't what just happened. The question is what happens next—and that answer is never in the last number you saw.

The streak ended on December 31, 2005—not because the strategy stopped working that day, but because that's when we stopped counting.

The streak ended on December 31, 2005—not because the strategy stopped working that day, but because that's when we stopped counting.

Chapter 2: The Year That Wasn't the Year

When was the last time you did your best work? Not this week—six months ago, nine months ago, the project you're still proud of but nobody seems to remember. Now ask yourself: when your manager writes your next performance review, which work do you think they'll remember?

She knew what was coming. She'd shipped two significant infrastructure improvements in February and March—the kind of work that prevents future disasters rather than fixing visible ones, which means almost nobody outside her immediate team would remember it happened. Then, in October, she'd picked up an urgent security patch that needed to ship fast, missed an edge case in testing, and the patch broke an internal tool that a VP happened to be using that day. Loudly. With witnesses.

The manager closed his laptop. "Overall," he said, "I think we need to talk about consistency."

Sarah had been consistent. Consistently good for ten months. Consistently visible in a bad way for one week in October. Guess which version made it into the written review?

That's recency bias in the wild. Not the academic definition. The thing itself, running in a real room with real consequences.

When Marissa Mayer brought stack ranking back to Yahoo in 2012, the policy got press for being ruthless. Forced distribution. Curve-grading. Cut the bottom ten percent. The headlines wrote themselves.

What the headlines missed—what most internal critics missed too, because they were focused on whether forced ranking was fair in principle—was the mechanism determining who actually landed in that bottom tier. It wasn't, as defenders claimed, an objective identification of true underperformers. It was a massive, company-wide amplification of whichever problems happened to surface in the eight weeks before review season opened.

A software engineer who'd shipped two major features in March and April but had a rocky sprint in October got cut. A product manager who'd quietly held a cross-functional team together for nine months but missed a Q4 deadline got marked for exit. The system claimed to measure a year. What it actually measured was whether your worst moment happened to land late.

Yahoo wasn't inventing a new problem. They were industrializing one that runs, quieter and less systematic but just as real, everywhere performance gets judged by human memory instead of by contemporaneous record.

The problem has a name in the industrial-organizational psychology literature, and the name does not hedge: *recency effect in performance appraisal*. It means exactly what it sounds like. The weeks closest to the review date exert a disproportionate influence on the final rating. Not because a manager consciously decided recent work matters more. Because recent work is *available* in memory in a way older work simply isn't anymore.

I know this pattern from the inside. Not just from reading the appraisal literature. From a mistake that cost me a client and taught me, the hard way, that recency isn't just a bias in how we remember the past—it's the lens through which we build our entire sense of what the evidence even is.

December 2014. I was managing a portfolio for a large institutional investor, the kind of client where a single account could make or break your year. I advised them to stay overweight in energy stocks. The recommendation wasn't reckless. It was built on what looked, at the time, like a clean story: the previous eighteen months had delivered double-digit returns in the sector. Everything I could see in the data I was looking at—prices, momentum indicators, recent earnings—suggested that trend had room to run. It felt like a solid call built on solid evidence.

Oil crashed two months later. The client left.

What I hadn't accounted for, because I genuinely didn't see it from inside the data window I was using, was that those eighteen months weren't "the trend." They were the tail end of a longer cycle. I would have needed a wider aperture to recognize it as a cycle at all. I'd mistaken recent data for the whole picture. Not because I was lazy. Not because I skipped the analysis. I did the work. I ran the numbers. I just did all of it on a sample that was dominated—completely—by what had happened most recently. Because recent data was what I could *see* most clearly. The older data, the context that would have complicated the story and maybe stopped me from making the call, had decayed in salience to the point where it wasn't competing for attention anymore.

Here's what made it worse: I had access to the full historical return series. I could have pulled it up. Widened the window. Forced myself to look at the longer pattern before making the call. The corrective information existed. I just didn't look, because what I could see most easily—what was most vivid, most recent, most *available*—felt like enough.

Recency didn't just tilt my judgment. It defined the entire evidentiary basis I was working from in the first place.

A manager sitting down to write a performance review in November doesn't even have that option. Unless the organization has built a real-time documentation system—brief notes logged throughout the year as events happen, not reconstructed from memory later—the full record of an employee's year doesn't exist anywhere outside the manager's head. And what exists in the manager's head by November is not a full record. It's a sharply uneven one, back-weighted toward whatever happened recently enough to still feel vivid.

An unaided human memory does not store a year as a year. It stores a scattered, uneven collection of moments, most of which decay steeply in the days and weeks after they happen. The ones that survive intact long enough to be retrieved in November—when the review form finally gets opened and the manager sits down to reconstruct twelve months of work—are not a representative sample of the full period. They're whichever moments happened recently enough, or were dramatic enough, to resist the ordinary fade.

A performance review that asks a manager to evaluate "the year" is asking for something memory can't deliver without help. What the manager ends up evaluating, in practice, is closer to the last two months, maybe three if there was a particularly vivid project earlier that burned itself in, plus a hazy and mostly generic sense that "the rest was fine" or "there were some issues earlier too, I think."

Let me show you what this looks like when it runs in an actual workplace, because the shape of it is common enough that you've probably seen some version of it yourself. Or lived through it.

An employee does solid, reliable work for ten months straight. Let's say it's a mid-level program manager—the kind of role where most of the work is coordinative and steady rather than punctuated by dramatic wins you'd remember individually. Nothing breaks. No one complains. Projects move forward on schedule. The work is exactly what "good performance" looks like in that role, which is to say it's largely invisible to anyone not directly involved in it. Competent coordination doesn't create visible friction or memorable crises. It just works.

Then, in month eleven, that same employee gets assigned to a high-stakes project on a short timeline. Something with executive visibility. Something where success or failure will be obvious and public.

And the employee either nails it or stumbles badly.

If the project goes well: the manager walks into the review with a vivid, recent, richly detailed memory of that eleventh-month win, and a thin, generic impression that "the rest of the year was solid too, I'm pretty sure." The review gets written. The rating skews high. The employee gets a strong raise, maybe a promotion.

If you asked the manager whether the rating was fair, the manager would say yes. The manager isn't lying. The manager is accurately reporting what the year *felt like* in retrospect.

But what the year felt like in retrospect is not the same thing as what actually happened across twelve months of work. It's a recency-weighted reconstruction that feels, from the inside, like a complete and even-handed memory. It isn't.

If the project goes badly: same mechanism, sharper consequences.

A single late-year stumble dominates the review. The employee, who spent ten months doing exactly what the role required, ends up rated as though the eleventh month were representative. The rating drops. The raise is smaller, or there isn't one. In more severe cases—and I've seen this happen more than once—that eleventh-month stumble becomes the first entry in a performance improvement plan. Or a data point in a layoff decision. Built on a sample of work that is genuinely unrepresentative of the full year's output but doesn't announce itself as unrepresentative to the person doing the remembering.

The manager isn't being dishonest. The manager has no conscious awareness of weighting recent evidence more heavily than older evidence. The distortion happens upstream of deliberate judgment—in what gets *retrieved* in the first place, before the careful reasoning about "what should this rating be" even starts.

And here's what makes this especially hard to see and fix: each individual review, looked at on its own, appears perfectly reasonable. A manager who rates an employee highly based substantially on one strong late-year project has produced a review that contains no obvious error. The project happened. It was strong. Crediting it seems fair.

The problem only shows up in aggregate. Across many employees and many review cycles, a pattern emerges that no single review would reveal: employees whose strong work happened to land late in the review period get systematically rated higher than employees whose equally strong work happened to land in February or March. Independent of total annual contribution.

That's not a hypothetical risk. That's the direct, mechanical consequence of asking unaided memory to do a job it is structurally incapable of doing fairly.

You might be thinking: okay, but managers can compensate for this, right? They know memory fades. They can deliberately try to remember the earlier months too.

They can try. It doesn't work.

There's a study—actually conducted in real performance review cycles, not a lab—that tracked managers who were explicitly warned about recency bias before they wrote reviews and asked to weight the full year evenly. The researchers then compared those reviews to a control group of managers who got no warning.

The warned group showed the exact same recency skew as the control group. Knowing about the bias didn't reduce it. Trying to compensate for it didn't work. Because the problem isn't that managers are forgetting to try to remember older events. The problem is that older events have genuinely faded in memory to the point where they aren't *available* to retrieve in the first place, no matter how hard you try.

You can't will yourself to remember something that's decayed past the point of retrieval. You can only work from what's actually still there. And what's still there, by November, is a sharply distorted sample.

Some organizations have figured this out, though usually not in the language of cognitive bias. They've just noticed, practically, that year-end reviews reconstructed from memory produce outcomes that don't square with what actually happened during the year. The fix they've landed on, when they've landed on one, is almost always some version of continuous documentation: regular check-ins, brief notes logged at the time an event happens rather than months later, a running record that doesn't rely on retrieval at all because it exists outside of memory entirely.

This isn't a minor procedural tweak. It's a completely different evidentiary basis for the review. A manager reading a note written in March is not trying to remember what happened in March. The manager is reading what actually happened, preserved at the time it happened, before decay had any chance to distort it. The review stops being "what does the manager currently find easiest to recall" and starts being "what actually occurred across the full period."

Those are—and this is the point of this entire chapter—frequently two very different things that get treated as the same review.

Adobe killed annual reviews entirely in 2012, replacing them with what they call "check-ins": brief, ongoing conversations between managers and employees throughout the year. Not because Adobe's executives had read the recency bias literature. Because they'd watched their annual review process produce results that senior leaders could see, just from pattern-matching across enough cycles, were systematically unfair. Employees whose strong work landed in Q1 or Q2 were getting lower ratings and smaller raises than employees whose strong work landed in Q4. Same quality of work. Different timing. Different outcomes.

The check-in system doesn't eliminate recency bias—nothing eliminates it, because you can't rewire how human memory decays. But it *compresses* the window. A conversation that happens every six weeks is drawing on six weeks of memory, not twelve months. The decay curve is still there, but it has less time to distort the sample before the record gets made.

Here's what happens when the distortion runs unchecked for long enough that employees start to notice it: they adjust.

Not consciously, maybe. Not in the language of cognitive bias. But they figure it out. They watch who got strong reviews. They notice those people had visible wins in the last quarter. And once you notice that, the rational response is to adjust your effort accordingly: coast a bit in the early and middle parts of the review period, then visibly ramp up output in the eight to ten weeks before the review is due. Front-load the last quarter with the kind of projects that are easy to describe and remember. Make sure your best work lands late.

This is not evidence that the employee is lazy or gaming the system in some underhanded way. It's evidence that the employee has correctly diagnosed the system's actual incentive structure and is responding to it rationally. The appraisal process rewards recency-timed effort. Employees learn to supply recency-timed effort.

And the organization ends up measuring—and compensating, and promoting—based on a pattern of work that has almost nothing to do with sustained, evenly distributed contribution across a full year.

What started as an unconscious bias in a manager's memory becomes, over enough cycles, a conscious and entirely defensible strategy on the part of the people being reviewed. Once that happens, the review has stopped measuring performance in any meaningful sense. It's measuring who best understood the game.

Microsoft ran a version of this for years under Steve Ballmer. The stack ranking system they used became a case study—business schools still teach it—in how incentive distortion compounds. Employees didn't just time their best work to land late in the review cycle. They actively avoided collaborating with high performers, because being on a team with someone likely to get ranked in the top tier meant someone else on that team had to get marked down. The curve was forced. If your teammate looked great in October, you were more likely to look average by comparison, even if your actual work was identical to what it had been all year.

The system claimed to identify and reward excellence. What it actually did was teach people to optimize for looking excellent in the narrow window that mattered, and to avoid situations where someone else's recent visibility might overshadow their own.

Satya Nadella killed stack ranking in 2013, one of his first moves as CEO. When he announced it, the internal reaction wasn't just relief—employees openly said they could finally go back to collaborating without worrying that helping a teammate might tank their own rating. That's not an exaggeration. That's what people actually said in the internal forums Microsoft made public later.

That's what happens when recency bias gets baked into a formal system. But you don't need a formal system for the distortion to run. It runs just as effectively, just more quietly, in the standard performance review most organizations use. No stack ranking required. Just a manager, a review form, and a year's worth of work that memory has compressed into a handful of vivid recent moments plus a vague sense that "the rest happened too, probably."

There's a further wrinkle here that makes the whole thing worse, and it shows up specifically in how organizations handle comparative reviews—the kind of calibration or ranking meetings where a group of managers get in a room together to reconcile their individual ratings before finalizing raises or promotions.

These meetings are designed, on paper, as a check against individual bias. The theory is that a room full of managers comparing notes should surface and correct any one manager's recency-skewed impression of a particular employee.

In practice, what often happens is that calibration meetings import the same distortion at a group level. Every manager in the room is working from the same kind of back-weighted, recency-shaped memory this chapter has been describing. A room full of independently biased judgments doesn't average out to an unbiased one. It produces a group consensus that everyone's last few weeks mattered most. And that consensus carries the additional and entirely unearned weight of having been "checked" by multiple people.

The distortion gets laundered, not corrected.

I sat in one of these meetings once. Mid-sized tech company, about forty employees up for review, six managers in the room. We were supposed to be reconciling ratings—making sure no one manager was grading too hard or too easy relative to the group.

One manager proposed a high rating for an engineer who'd shipped a major feature in late October. Another manager, who'd worked with the same engineer on a different project back in March, said, "Wait, I thought we agreed in the spring that he was solid but not exceptional?"

First manager paused. "Yeah, I mean... I think he's grown a lot since then."

Had he? Maybe. Or maybe the March impression had faded and the October project was vivid and the growth narrative was a story we told ourselves to reconcile the two without having to admit we were just remembering October more clearly.

We went with the high rating. It felt fair. It might have been fair. But the evidence we were working from was not a complete record of the year. It was six people's overlapping, decayed, October-heavy memories dressed up as a thorough review.

The stakes get higher when you move from annual reviews to promotion decisions, because promotions are less frequent, less easily reversed, and typically rely on a different evidentiary process. A promotion case, in most organizations that have a formal process for this at all, is built around a written packet: a compilation of accomplishments, project summaries, peer endorsements, and manager narratives assembled specifically to make the case for advancement.

This might look, at first glance, like exactly the kind of contemporaneous record this chapter has been arguing for. It's written down. It's detailed. It's not just unaided recall.

But in practice, promotion packets often reproduce the same recency distortion in a different form. The person assembling the packet—usually the employee's manager, sometimes the employee themselves—is drawing on the same decayed, back-weighted memory this chapter has described throughout. The accomplishments that feel most compelling to feature, the projects that are easiest to describe persuasively, tend to be the ones that happened recently enough to still be vivid.

The packet ends up looking, to a promotion committee reading it cold, like a comprehensive case built on a full tenure. What it often is: a case built substantially on the last six to nine months, retroactively framed as representative of a much longer stretch the packet's author simply had less clear material available to pull from.

This creates a specific and somewhat perverse incentive around promotion timing itself. An employee who has done strong, sustained work for three years but happens to be in a relatively quiet period in the months leading up to a promotion cycle is structurally disadvantaged. Not compared to an employee with better total contribution. Compared to an employee with a shorter but more recently concentrated record of visible achievement.

The second employee's case isn't stronger on the merits. It's *easier to assemble* from vivid, recently available material.

Once employees notice this—and they do notice, usually after watching one promotion cycle and seeing who advanced—they adjust. The next time a promotion window opens, they make sure their biggest, most visible projects land in the immediate run-up.

This is, again, a completely rational response to the system as it actually operates. And it further degrades the system's ability to identify and reward the thing it was nominally built to reward: sustained high performance over time, not well-timed high performance in a narrow window.

The recency effect also shows up, in a particularly consequential way, in how organizations handle underperformance. The decision to put someone on a formal improvement plan, or in more severe cases to terminate employment, is supposed to be based on a documented *pattern* of underperformance. Not a single incident. The documentation requirement exists in part as a safeguard against exactly the kind of recency-driven overreaction this chapter has been describing.

But the safeguard only works if the documentation itself was gathered evenly across the full period under review. Not gathered disproportionately in response to a recent, salient problem that finally prompted a manager to start building a file.

Here's what that looks like in practice, and I've seen this play out more than once:

An employee makes a visible, public mistake. A demo that crashes in front of executives. A customer complaint that escalates to the VP level. A missed deadline on something the CEO was tracking.

The manager, who had not been documenting concerns before—because there weren't any particularly vivid ones to document—suddenly starts paying closer attention and writing things down. The manager then *also* reaches back into memory to reconstruct earlier incidents that, in hindsight and in light of the recent mistake, now seem like they might have been warning signs. Those earlier incidents get added to the file retroactively.

The file grows. It starts to look like a pattern. And because it's a written file, it carries the weight of documentation. Even though the documentation process itself began only after the recency-triggered event that prompted the scrutiny in the first place.

The formal safeguard—requiring a documented pattern rather than a snap judgment—ends up reproducing the recency distortion it was designed to prevent. The pattern was constructed using the same decayed, unevenly available memory the safeguard was supposed to correct for.

A documentation habit that starts in response to a recent problem, rather than running evenly from an employee's first day, will systematically overrepresent the recent period in the file. That's the period during which documentation was actually happening. Everything before that gets reconstructed selectively, if it gets included at all. And reconstruction is exactly the process we know, from everything this chapter has covered, to be unreliable.

The employee in this scenario hasn't necessarily gotten worse. The scrutiny has gotten sharper, triggered by one salient recent event, and now everything the employee does is being viewed through the lens of that event. Mistakes that would have been shrugged off in March—minor enough not to make it into memory at all—are now getting written down in November because the manager is actively looking for a pattern and memory is more than happy to supply confirmatory evidence.

This is how people get fired for being unlucky in their timing.

Here's the piece that makes all of this harder than just saying "document everything evenly": there *is* a version of this where recent performance should count more.

People genuinely do improve. People genuinely do learn. An employee who struggled during a rough onboarding in January and February, then genuinely mastered the role by October, is not being unfairly flattered by a review that gives significant weight to the October-level competence. That review is tracking a real trajectory. The recent evidence is the more informative evidence.

The distinction that matters—and the one an appraisal system needs to be able to make deliberately rather than leaving to managerial instinct—is between recency that reflects a real, sustained change in capability and recency that reflects one memorable but unrepresentative episode sitting on top of an otherwise stable baseline.

The first kind deserves extra weight.

The second kind needs to be recognized for what it is: a single data point that memory's architecture has dressed up to look like the whole story.

Distinguishing between those two in practice requires exactly the thing unaided memory is worst at: comparing the recent episode against a clear, evenly resolved picture of what the earlier months actually looked like. A manager can't make that judgment responsibly without a full record to compare against. And a full record is precisely what recency bias prevents from forming in memory in the first place.

You're stuck. Unless you build the record outside of memory.

That's the fix. Not "try harder to remember the full year." Not "be aware of recency bias and compensate for it mentally." Those don't work. The research is clear on this. Awareness doesn't reduce the bias. Trying to compensate for it manually, in your head, doesn't work either. The decay has already happened. The distortion is already baked into what's available to retrieve.

The fix is to stop relying on retrieval entirely.

Document as you go. Not at review time. Not when something goes wrong. As events happen. Brief notes. Enough detail that six months later you can read the note and remember what actually occurred, not what you think probably occurred based on your current impression of the person.

This doesn't have to be elaborate. A few sentences per week. "Shipped X feature on time, handled Y stakeholder pushback well, missed Z deadline but flagged it early and proposed a workaround." Written when it happens. Not reconstructed later.

When November comes and the review form opens, you're not asking your memory to do something it can't do. You're reading a record that was made at the time, before decay had a chance to distort it. The review stops being "what do I currently find easiest to recall" and starts being "what actually occurred across the full period."

That shift—from reconstructed memory to contemporaneous record—is the entire difference between a review process that systematically advantages employees whose strong work happened to land late and a review process that actually measures performance across the full year.

Most organizations don't do this. Not because they've tried it and found it too burdensome. Because they haven't tried it at all. They're still operating on the assumption that a manager's memory in November is a reliable guide to what happened in March. It isn't. It never was. And every year that assumption runs uncorrected, it produces outcomes that are unfair in ways the people producing them genuinely don't see, because the distortion happens upstream of conscious judgment.

You can't fix a system by asking people to try harder within the system's existing constraints. You fix it by changing the constraints. Stop asking memory to do a job it can't do. Build the record outside of memory. Make the record contemporaneous. Make it even across the full period, not back-loaded in response to recent events.

Do that, and the recency effect doesn't disappear—you can't rewire how human memory works—but it stops determining who gets promoted, who gets fired, and who gets paid for work the organization has already forgotten they did.

The question to ask yourself, whether you're the person writing the review or the person being reviewed, is this: what evidentiary basis is this judgment actually built on? A full record of the year? Or a decayed, back-weighted, October-heavy memory that feels like a full record because memory doesn't announce its own gaps?

If you don't have a clear answer—if the review process you're in doesn't produce contemporaneous documentation that you can point to and say, "that's what actually happened, preserved at the time it happened"—then you're not measuring the year.

You're measuring the last few months, dressed up to look like the year, and hoping no one notices the difference.

Forty minutes of scrolling through twelve months of work, compressed into the projects from the last quarter. The manager started typing.

Chapter 3: The Last Witness

Johnnie Cochran spoke for three hours and forty minutes. He saved 'If it doesn't fit, you must acquit' for the last seven minutes.

He saved "If it doesn't fit, you must acquit" for the last seven minutes.

Not the opening. Not scattered through the middle. The absolute last thing twelve jurors heard before walking into deliberation on October 2, 1995, was a rhyme about a glove that didn't fit O.J. Simpson's hand when he tried to pull it on in front of them.

Everything else came before that moment. DNA evidence so cutting-edge most Americans had never heard of it outside this trial. Blood spatter patterns analyzed by experts who'd spent decades studying how blood moves through air, how it lands on fabric, what the spray pattern tells you about where someone was standing when the knife went in. A timeline reconstructed down to individual minutes. A documented history of domestic violence spanning years: 911 calls you could listen to in Nicole Brown Simpson's own voice, photographs of her bruised face taken by police, witness after witness describing incidents they'd seen firsthand. Months of testimony.

And then Cochran stood up.

By the time he sat down, all that prior evidence—not erased, not disproven, but simply *earlier*—had been pushed backward in the jury's working memory by the sheer fact that Cochran's argument came last. When those twelve people walked into deliberation the next morning, what sat most clearly in their minds wasn't the DNA. Wasn't the blood evidence. Wasn't the 911 tapes. It was the defense's closing. The glove. The rhyme.

The verdict came back in less than four hours.

I'm not relitigating whether they got it right. What I'm pointing to is how the structure of a trial privileges certain information over other information purely through the order in which that information arrives. Independent of strength. Independent of truth. A trial is a scheduling problem before it's anything else. Someone decides what gets presented when. That order shapes what jurors remember most clearly, which shapes what they weight most heavily, which shapes the verdict.

None of this is accidental. None of it is neutral. And none of it stays contained inside courtrooms.

I spent most of my twenties believing I was making decisions based on evidence. I'd pull up a stock's chart—three months of steady upward momentum, every article from the past month pointing in the same direction, analyst upgrades stacking up—and I'd call that research.

What I was actually doing was letting the most recent information crowd out everything that came before it, and mistaking the vividness of recent data for reliability.

Same mechanism. Different courtroom.

I watched positions I'd held for six months, positions that had been slowly, steadily building value, and blew them up in a single afternoon because the price dropped two days in a row and suddenly all I could remember was those two days. The previous six months? Gone. Not literally gone—I could've pulled up the chart if I'd tried. But they weren't *present* in my mind when I made the decision to sell. What was present was the last 48 hours. The drop. The fear.

I sold near the bottom. Watched the price recover a week later. Watched it climb for another eighteen months while I sat on the sidelines, too embarrassed to buy back in at a higher price than where I'd sold.

That single pattern, repeated across dozens of positions over maybe three years, cost me more money than every genuinely bad company I ever bought. The bad companies were identifiable mistakes—I picked wrong, I missed something, fine. But this? I wasn't learning, because I didn't understand I was doing it. Every single time, in the moment, the decision felt rational. Evidence-based. The recent data was *right there*. How could I ignore it?

What I couldn't see was that I was running the same cognitive process as those twelve jurors in 1995, privileging the last thing I'd seen to a degree that had nothing to do with how predictive it actually was.

You might be thinking: you just said you *could've* pulled up the full chart. You had access to the longer history. So what's the excuse?

Fair point. But having information *available* and actually *weighting it appropriately* are not the same thing.

A jury can ask for transcripts during deliberation. They can review exhibits. They spend hours, sometimes days, working through the evidence together. All of that should, in theory, blunt the raw recency effect.

It does blunt it. It doesn't eliminate it.

Researchers who study jury decision-making have found that the order of testimony continues to shape which evidence jurors weight most heavily even after you account for notes, transcripts, and extended deliberation. The position of a piece of evidence in the trial's sequence affects how persuasive jurors find it, separate from the content itself.

Not because jurors are dumb. Not because they're lazy. But because memory is not a recording device. It's a reconstruction. And reconstruction, every single time, favors whatever requires the least effort to rebuild.

Hermann Ebbinghaus—working alone in the 1880s, running experiments on himself because he couldn't get funding to study anyone else—spent years memorizing lists of nonsense syllables and tracking what stuck. The pattern showed up immediately.

Show someone a list of words, one after another. Then ask them to recall it.

The first few words come back easily. The last few words come back easily. Everything in the middle? Gone.

This is the serial position effect. The early advantage is called primacy—those items got more rehearsal, had time to transfer into long-term storage. The late advantage is recency. Those items are still sitting in short-term memory when you test recall. They haven't faded yet.

Ebbinghaus published this work in 1885. It's been replicated hundreds of times since. We've known about it for longer than we've known about relativity. Longer than we've known about DNA.

And yet.

I watch professional investors—people who know this research, who could explain the serial position effect better than I just did—make the exact same mistake I was making in my twenties. Because knowing about a bias and successfully correcting for it are two completely different problems, and the second one is way harder.

There's a study where researchers presented people with arguments on a contentious political topic. Same arguments. Same participants. The only thing that changed was the order in which strong arguments versus weak arguments appeared.

Result? The exact same argument was rated as more persuasive when it came late than when it came early.

Nothing about the content changed. The position changed. The persuasiveness rating changed with it.

If that happens with abstract policy arguments in a controlled university setting where nobody has money on the line, it absolutely happens with testimony in a courtroom where someone's freedom is at stake. And it absolutely happens with market data when your retirement account is on the line and you're staring at a position that's down 15% in three days.

The stakes make it worse, not better. The more you care about getting the decision right, the more your brain defaults to the easiest available heuristic—and the easiest heuristic is always "what happened most recently?"

Picture a civil trial. The plaintiff is suing for enough money that losing means bankruptcy. Five witnesses over three days.

The first witness is an expert. Forensic accountant. He spent two months analyzing the defendant's financial records and he's getting paid fifteen thousand dollars to show up and explain what he found. He's testified maybe thirty times before and he understands how to walk a jury through complex material without losing them.

For ninety minutes he takes them through a reconstruction of financial fraud: shell companies registered in Delaware with no listed address, wire transfers that don't match the amounts on the invoices, ledgers that were altered after the fact, timestamps on digital files that prove certain documents were backdated. He's got exhibits. He's got charts. He's got a timeline.

Most of the jurors are taking notes as fast as they can write. Some of them are clearly lost by minute twenty—that glazed look people get when the details are coming too fast.

By the time deliberation starts two days later—forty-eight hours and four more witnesses downstream—nobody in that jury room can reconstruct what the forensic accountant said with any detail. It gets summarized as "something about the financial records." A vague outline. Effectively discounted, not because he was wrong, not because his analysis was flawed, but because he testified first and the clarity has bled out of it. What remains is a general sense that "the numbers looked bad," which is nowhere near as persuasive as the specific, step-by-step demonstration he actually delivered.

The three middle witnesses blur together even worse. One of them gave important testimony—a former employee who described a conversation she overheard in the break room, the defendant telling someone on the phone that he knew the deal was fraudulent but he was going through with it anyway—but none of what those three said was dramatic enough to anchor a vivid memory. And none of them testified recently enough to still be sitting in short-term recall when deliberation begins.

They're not forgotten. They're hazy.

When a juror tries to remember what Witness Three said, the reconstruction is effortful. Incomplete. So mostly, in deliberation, they don't try. They focus on what they can remember clearly without work.

The fifth witness testified late on the final afternoon. Eight minutes of testimony. Emotionally vivid. She was a neighbor who'd watched this whole situation unfold over the course of a year. She spoke in plain language. No jargon, no technical terms. She just talked about a single moment when she saw the defendant do the thing the plaintiff says he did.

She cried on the stand. Not a breakdown—just, she teared up, took a breath, kept going. Made eye contact with the jury the whole time.

When deliberation begins the next morning, her testimony dominates immediately.

Why?

Not because the jurors collectively decided hers was the most reliable or most probative evidence. Because it's the testimony every single person in that room can reconstruct most easily and most completely without effort. The forensic accountant's ninety-minute rigorous breakdown—potentially the strongest evidence in the case—gets maybe two sentences in deliberation.

"He said the records were altered."

"Yeah, something about the dates didn't match."

That's it. That's all ninety minutes reduces to.

The final witness's eight-minute account gets twenty minutes of discussion. Not because it earned that on its merits. Because it's what everyone can actually remember.

The jury's verdict reflects a version of the trial that never existed as presented. In the version they're working from—the version reconstructed after two days has been filtered through the serial position effect—that brief final testimony carries weight equal to or exceeding everything that came before it. Purely because of when she happened to take the stand.

You ask those jurors afterward why they ruled the way they did, and not one of them will say "because she testified last." They'll cite substance. They'll say she was credible. Direct. Sincere. They won't say—because they genuinely don't know—that timing made her *feel* more persuasive relative to everything they heard earlier.

The bias never announces itself. It just does its work quietly, underneath the deliberation, shaping which evidence feels most salient without ever becoming visible as a factor in the decision.

You might be thinking: that's jurors. Jurors don't have Bloomberg terminals. They can't pull up a ten-year chart whenever they want. They're working from memory because memory is all they've got.

True.

Except when I watch someone—including myself, especially myself—make an actual buy or sell decision in real time, the process looks a lot more like that jury deliberation than anyone wants to admit.

You've got years of data theoretically available. You could pull up a decade of price history in about four seconds. But what dominates the decision? What you looked at most recently. What felt most vivid. What required the least mental effort to reconstruct.

The earnings beat from last week. The analyst upgrade from yesterday. The price action from this morning.

The chart from five years ago that shows this exact setup failing three times in a row? That takes work to retrieve. You'd have to actively decide to look for it. And most of the time, in the moment, you don't. Because what's right in front of you feels sufficient.

I cannot tell you how many times I've made a trade, had it go wrong, and then—while doing the post-mortem—discovered that the exact thing I missed was sitting right there in the historical data the whole time. Not hidden. Not obscure. Just not recent enough to be sitting in my active memory when I made the decision.

And the feeling you get when you realize that?

It's worse than losing money on a company that turned out to be fraudulent. Way worse. Because at least with fraud, you can tell yourself the information wasn't available, you got lied to, there was no way to know. But this? You *did* know. You just didn't remember at the right time.

That's the cost. Not just money. But also confidence. The ability to trust your own judgment. Because every time you find that the information was right there and you just didn't use it, it reinforces this feeling that you can't rely on yourself to make good decisions even when you have everything you need.

Trial attorneys know this. They may not know the term "serial position effect"—most of them don't—but they know you save your strongest witness for last. Both sides fight for the most favorable position in the sequence. The closing argument itself is positioned to be the very last thing jurors hear before deliberation begins.

Nobody inside the legal profession calls this "exploiting a cognitive bias." It's called good trial craft. An intuition built up over generations of courtroom practice that order matters as much as content, maybe more. The formal psychological research mostly just confirmed what trial lawyers already knew from experience.

What makes this worth examining carefully is the gap between what the legal system *claims* to value and what its structure actually rewards.

The formal rules say jurors should weigh testimony on substance. Consistency with other evidence. Corroboration. Credibility. Nowhere in the jury instructions does timing appear as a legitimate factor. The instructions assume jurors can reconstruct the entire trial with equal clarity no matter when each piece was presented.

But order shapes weight. Through a mechanism operating entirely below conscious awareness.

A juror who's been disproportionately influenced by that final witness's testimony will cite substance if you ask them to explain their reasoning. They'll say she was credible. Direct. Sincere. They won't say—because they genuinely don't know—that timing made her *feel* more persuasive.

The bias does its work invisibly. It shapes the outcome without ever becoming visible as part of the process.

This gap—between the system's stated values and its actual structure—is why order effects are almost impossible to appeal.

You can appeal because evidence was improperly admitted. You can appeal because a witness was

The jury deliberated for four hours. They remembered the last seven minutes better than the first three months.

Chapter 4: The Career Year

The Angels cap didn't fit right. Not yet. On December 8, 2011, Albert Pujols stood at a podium in Anaheim wearing red that belonged to someone else, holding a pen above a $240 million contract. That contract wasn't buying a career. It was buying one season—the one that had just ended.

What nobody said at that press conference—what would have sounded like showing up to a wedding to read the divorce statistics—was that the Angels had almost certainly just bought the top.

Pujols never hit 40 home runs again. His batting average never touched .300 again. By year five of the contract he was a below-average hitter. By the end he was coming off the bench. The Angels spent an entire decade trying to build a championship roster around a player whose peak performance, the performance that justified a quarter-billion-dollar commitment, had already happened before the contract existed.

Here's what that decade actually looked like, if you're willing to sit with it for a minute: Mike Trout—arguably the best player in baseball—entered his prime surrounded by pieces that should have built a dynasty. The Angels had pitching. They had talent. What they didn't have was the payroll flexibility to put those pieces together, because they'd committed $24 million a year to a first baseman whose production was sliding backward while the contract ran forward.

The Angels made the playoffs once in those ten years. Once. With Mike Trout.

That's not just money. That's a career. Multiple careers, actually—Trout's, the other players who could have been there, the coaches who got fired trying to make it work with one hand tied behind their back. The what-could-have-been that you can't get back because the decision you made off one season's worth of data locked you into a decade you can't exit.

I need to be honest about something here: I've watched this pattern repeat so many times across different domains that I've started to think of it as one of the most expensive cognitive traps we fall into. And I've fallen into it myself. Not with baseball contracts—I don't have that kind of money, and neither do you, probably—but with the underlying mechanism. The belief that what just happened is more real than everything that came before. That momentum tells you where something's going rather than just where it's been.

Professional sports organizations keep more granular statistical data on their players than almost any other industry keeps on its workforce. Decades of game logs. Injury histories. Age curves showing the typical performance arc across a career—rising through the twenties, peaking around twenty-seven or twenty-eight, declining after. Situational splits down to left-handed pitchers on Tuesday nights. All of it searchable, all of it theoretically capable of grounding every contract decision in a player's full career arc instead of just the slice you saw last season.

And yet.

A player performs at or near career-best levels in the season immediately before free agency. A team signs that player to a long-term deal priced to that peak. The player then—almost inevitably—regresses. Sometimes gradually. Sometimes off a cliff. But the reversion comes. The industry even has a name for it: the walk-year effect.

You might be thinking this is just hindsight. Easy to spot the pattern after it happens, harder to see it coming when you're the one writing the check. And you'd be right to push back on that—except the pattern is so well-established that front-office executives make jokes about it. They call it the "contract year phenomenon." They write about it in trade publications. They build statistical models specifically to detect it.

Then they sign the contracts anyway.

The mechanism underneath all this is mean reversion, which sounds like statistics-class vocabulary until you see it take a decade of someone's career. Athletic performance, like investment returns, varies year to year around a player's true underlying ability. Any single season reflects some mix of genuine talent and ordinary variance: health, matchup luck, slight changes in role, the random physics of a ball coming off a bat.

A player's best season almost by definition sits at the favorable extreme of that variance. It's the year where everything broke right.

The seasons that follow are far more likely to drift back toward the player's career average than to sustain the peak. Not because the player stopped trying. Not because something broke. Just because that's what variance does when you drew the good end of it once. You got heads seven times in a row, and now the coin remembers it's supposed to be fifty-fifty.

Except the coin never forgot. You just thought the streak meant something it didn't.

Sports analysts have documented this so thoroughly it now counts as front-office common knowledge. The regression pattern isn't a secret. The corrective knowledge is sitting right there.

What fails is not access to the data. What fails is the process by which that data competes, inside an actual negotiation, against the immediate, vivid, freshly-observed evidence of a player who just spent an entire season performing at an extraordinary level in front of the very people about to sign the check.

Picture the mechanics. A general manager sits in a conference room with the team's scouting staff and analytics department. They're evaluating a contract offer for a player entering free agency. The player's statistics across five prior seasons show solid production—useful regular, not a star. Then comes the sixth season, and the numbers spike. Twenty percent better, maybe thirty. Driven by some blend of genuine improvement, favorable matchups, and variance that nobody in the room can cleanly separate because the tools aren't precise enough and one season is, statistically speaking, tissue-paper-thin evidence of permanent change.

The analytics staff would describe the situation accurately if you asked them in the abstract. One strong season is weak evidence of a skill jump. The five-year baseline is the better predictor. Basic statistics.

But this is not an abstract exercise.

This meeting happens after a season the entire organization just watched unfold in real time, game by game, highlight by highlight. Each strong performance added another vivid, easily-retrieved memory to the room's collective impression of the player. The five prior seasons of solid-but-unspectacular work sit further back in everyone's mind, blurred together the way an employee's February accomplishments blur by December when you're writing the year-end review.

The recent season doesn't need to win the argument on the data's terms. It's already won the argument for attention before anyone opens their mouth.

The contract that follows gets priced closer to the recent peak than the career baseline would justify. Not because anyone stood up and made an identifiably irrational claim. But because the group's shared impression has shifted, collectively and mostly invisibly, toward the most available evidence rather than the most representative evidence.

They're not paying for what the player has demonstrated on average. They're paying for what happened most recently, priced as if that season were a new permanent level rather than a favorable draw from the same distribution the player's always occupied.

And here's where it gets expensive.

A long-term sports contract is a multi-year commitment that becomes a sunk cost the instant it's signed. An investor who realizes a mutual fund is reverting to mediocrity can sell next week. A team locked into a ten-year deal is stuck regardless of how fast the reversion arrives. So the walk-year mistake doesn't merely cost one bad season. It compounds across the entire length of the contract, constraining roster flexibility and payroll allocation for years. Making it vastly more expensive to unwind than the equivalent error in a liquid market.

The Pujols contract didn't just cost the Angels money. It cost them their window.

Let that sit for a second. One of the greatest players in the history of the sport spent his entire twenties on a team that couldn't build around him because they'd bet a quarter-billion dollars on one season of data from a player in his thirties. That's not just an accounting error. That's a career—actually, it's the loss of what should have been several Hall of Fame careers playing together in a way we'll never get to see now.

Think about what that decade felt like if you were in it. Not as a fan watching from the stands, but as one of the people living inside the decision. You're a coach whose job depends on winning games with a roster you didn't build and can't fix because the money's already spoken for. You're a young player watching your prime years tick by on a team that's one piece away from contending but can never afford that piece. You're the GM who has to go into the owner's office every April and explain why this year won't be different, knowing the reason is a decision you made—or inherited—years ago that you're now locked into watching play out in slow motion.

That's the cost I want you to feel. Not the dollar figure. The lost years.

Some organizations have built institutional counterweights, and the shape these take is worth paying attention to because they're rare enough that when they work, they stand out. Analytically sophisticated front offices now construct valuation models that deliberately weight multi-year baselines more heavily than the most recent season by design. Not because the recent season is uninformative—it isn't. But because building the discount into the model's structure before any specific negotiation begins removes the decision from the room's in-the-moment, recency-vulnerable judgment.

The rule gets set in advance, when no specific player's vivid recent performance is sitting there distorting it.

This is the same logic behind pre-registered decision criteria in other contexts this book will return to: a standard set before the emotionally salient evidence arrives is considerably harder for that evidence to bend than a judgment formed in the moment the evidence is freshest and most alive in your head.

But here's the wrinkle, and I think this is where the real resistance to fixing this problem lives. The cost of following such a model isn't purely financial, and this explains why even organizations that know better sometimes override their own recommendations.

An executive who declines to pay premium money for a player coming off a standout season, citing regression-to-baseline, is making a call that will look to fans, media, and ownership like a failure to recognize obvious talent. Especially in the seasons right after, before any reversion becomes visible.

The executive who overpays, by contrast, makes a decision that gets praised in the short term regardless of long-term accuracy, because everyone else is also weighting the recent evidence heavily. The overpayment looks sound. Conservative, even. The underpayment looks cheap.

So correctly discounting a recent hot streak carries real social and career risk even when the statistical reasoning is unimpeachable.

Billy Beane—if you've seen *Moneyball* you know the name, if you haven't I'm about to tell you why it matters—built his entire reputation in part by resisting this pattern. Beane let players walk in free agency after career years that other teams bid up. He got destroyed in the local press for it. Fans accused him of being cheap, of not caring about winning, of running a farm system for richer clubs.

Then those players regressed with their new teams while Oakland replaced them for a fraction of the cost.

Beane's approach was vindicated, but the vindication took years. And he spent those years being called a fool by people who were looking only at the most recent season and couldn't see what he saw in the full distribution. The social cost of being right later is that you look wrong now, and "now" is when you're getting evaluated. By your boss. By the media. By the fans who pay for tickets.

That asymmetry—the biased decision being socially cheap and the debiased decision being socially expensive, at least in the short run—is not unique to baseball front offices. It's why an entire industry can know about a bias, publish research quantifying it, build models to correct for it, and still watch the same overpayment pattern repeat season after season.

Knowledge of a bias reduces neither the vividness of the evidence that triggers it nor the social cost of resisting it when everyone around you is swimming in the same current.

The pattern doesn't stop at contract negotiations. It shows up in the in-season decisions coaches make about who plays and who sits. A player who performs exceptionally well across a handful of recent games gets an expanded role, a more prominent spot in the lineup, the ball in the decisive final possession—chosen over a player with a stronger season-long record but a less vivid recent stretch.

Coaches call this "riding the hot hand."

And there's been a small mountain of research into whether streaks in individual performance reflect temporarily elevated ability or just the ordinary clustering you get in any random sequence. The research literature on this went through some messy revisions—early work was widely read as debunking the hot hand as pure illusion, people seeing patterns in noise. Later studies using more refined methods found some genuine short-term streak effects in specific contexts. The question's still contested in the academic journals.

But what's not contested is the behavioral fact this chapter cares about: coaches, teammates, and fans consistently overestimate how much a short recent streak should update their expectations for what comes next, regardless of how much genuine signal that streak actually contains.

The dollar consequences are smaller than a multi-year contract, but the effect on outcomes is real. A coaching decision made under the influence of a recent hot streak is a miniature version of the same walk-year mistake, just repeated at a faster cadence. Game to game. Possession to possession.

A player benched despite a strong career track record because a recent slump is the most vivid thing in the coach's memory is experiencing the same mechanism you experience when a late-year stumble dominates an otherwise strong annual review. The domain changed from office to locker room. The distortion is identical.

I want to pause here and acknowledge something, because I think you might be forming an objection right about now. You might be thinking: isn't recent performance at least somewhat more predictive than old performance? If a player's been trending up, shouldn't that matter?

Yes. Sometimes. When there's a genuine developmental arc—a young player entering their prime, a veteran making a real mechanical adjustment—recent performance can signal a new level.

The problem is we're terrible at distinguishing that signal from noise in real time.

A twenty-eight-year-old having a career year and a thirty-two-year-old having a career year look identical on the stat sheet. One might be a player hitting their peak and sustaining it. The other is almost certainly variance about to revert. The base rates say the thirty-two-year-old is aging, not ascending.

But the recent season makes both cases feel equally real, equally like the player you should be betting on, because both just did the thing right in front of you.

That's the trap. We don't actually believe the recent data is more predictive. We believe it's more *real*. It feels safer to trust what we just watched than to admit we're making a probabilistic guess based on a noisy baseline. Momentum is the only pattern we can see clearly in the moment, which is exactly why it's the most dangerous thing to bet on.

Let me tell you about a decision I made that I'm still not entirely sure was wrong, even though I know the reasoning behind it was. A few years ago I was evaluating someone for a senior role on a project I was running. This person had a solid track record—consistently good work over several years, nothing spectacular but reliable, the kind of contributor you're always glad to have on the team. Then, in the six months leading up to the hiring decision, they produced work that was genuinely exceptional. Creative, insightful, ahead of schedule. The kind of work that makes you think you're seeing someone step into a new level of capability.

I gave them the role. And for about four months, the work continued at that elevated level. Then it started drifting back. Not bad—still solid, still the reliable contributor they'd always been. Just not the exceptional work I'd seen in those decisive six months before the decision.

Looking back now, I can see exactly what happened. I weighted those recent six months far more heavily than the several years that came before. I treated the peak as the new baseline instead of what it probably was: a stretch where everything aligned favorably and they were working at the top of their variance. The person didn't change. My expectations did, because I mistook a favorable sample for a permanent shift.

The thing is, I'm still not sure I'd make a different decision if I had to do it again. Because in the moment, with the information I had access to and the way my brain naturally processes vivid recent evidence versus blurred historical patterns, that recent performance felt more real than the years of solid-but-unspectacular work. It felt like the truth about who this person was becoming, not a temporary deviation from who they'd always been.

That's what this chapter is actually about. Not whether we should pay attention to recent evidence—we should. But whether we can build systems and processes that protect us from our own tendency to treat recent evidence as if it's more real than it actually is.

The clearest dividing line between organizations that have built resistance to the walk-year pattern and those that keep repeating it is rarely access to data. Nearly every professional franchise now has access to broadly similar statistical tools.

The real difference is organizational process: who holds final decision authority, and how insulated that authority is from the emotionally vivid, in-the-room experience of having just watched a standout season unfold.

Front offices that have institutionalized a formal, documented valuation step—a model output that must be explicitly overridden, in writing, with a stated justification—create exactly the friction the earlier chapters described. The friction doesn't eliminate the temptation to overpay for a recent peak. It doesn't need to. It simply requires that anyone choosing to override the model's conservative, full-record-based recommendation do so consciously and on the record.

Converting a decision that would otherwise happen invisibly, shaped by whatever's most vivid in the room, into a decision that must be defended explicitly against the very standard it's departing from.

Organizations that skip this step, relying instead on informal in-room consensus when a contract gets negotiated, show no comparable friction. The walk-year pattern recurs in their transaction history with a regularity the organizations with the formal override step don't share.

You can see it in the data, if you go looking. Teams with strong analytics departments that lack authority show the same contract mistakes as teams with no analytics at all. Having the right answer in the room doesn't matter if the room isn't set up to act on it.

And here's what that looks like in practice, because I think it's worth getting specific about the mechanics: An organization implements a formal valuation model. Before any contract negotiation begins, the model outputs a recommended contract value based on the player's multi-year baseline performance, adjusted for age and position. That number gets written down and dated.

When the actual negotiation happens—when the player's agent is in the room, when the most recent season's highlights are fresh in everyone's mind, when the pressure to "get the deal done" is highest—the model's recommendation is still sitting there on paper. If the final offer exceeds that recommendation by more than a set threshold, someone has to write a memo explaining why. Not to kill the deal. Just to document that the organization is consciously choosing to depart from its own standard, and why that departure is justified in this specific case.

That's it. That's the entire intervention. And it works, not because it prevents bad decisions, but because it makes them visible.

Most walk-year overpayments happen invisibly. Nobody in the room is consciously thinking "I'm going to ignore this player's career baseline and price this contract to their peak season even though I know that's probably variance." They're thinking "this is what it takes to get this caliber of player" while their brain quietly does the work of treating the recent season as more representative than it is.

The written override requirement doesn't stop that mental process. But it forces the final decision through a step where the gap between the model's recommendation and the actual offer becomes visible and must be justified. And justifying a decision—putting words on paper that explain why you're departing from the standard—activates a different kind of thinking than the in-the-moment impression-based judgment that would otherwise prevail.

You can't write "because the recent season felt really impressive" in the memo. You have to articulate a reason that sounds defensible when read later. Which means you have to either find evidence that this really is a genuine developmental arc rather than variance, or admit you don't have that evidence and you're overriding anyway.

Both are allowed. But making the choice explicit changes the frequency with which organizations choose the override.

The pattern reaches beyond player contracts into coaching retention, and this is where the human cost of the bias gets even starker because it's not just money and roster flexibility at stake—it's people's careers and reputations.

A coaching tenure typically spans several seasons of widely varying team performance, shaped by factors well outside the coach's control: roster talent inherited from prior regimes, injuries, division strength, front-office roster moves the coach never asked for.

A fair evaluation would need to isolate the coach's effect from all that surrounding noise across a multi-year sample large enough to average out the variance any team's record naturally contains.

What organizations actually do, especially under pressure from ownership or an angry fan base, is evaluate a coach substantially on the most recent season's record. Sometimes the most recent several games. They treat a short, recent, noisy sample as if it were a clean signal of underlying competence, the same way the chapter's opening case treated a single standout season as if it reliably signaled a player's true ability level going forward.

Lovie Smith coached the Chicago Bears for nine seasons. He won the NFC Championship in 2006, took the team to the Super Bowl. Posted a winning record in six of his nine years. His career record with Chicago was 81-63. By any full-career measure, a successful tenure.

In 2012, after one 10-6 season that missed the playoffs, the Bears fired him.

The decision was made almost entirely on the strength of the most recent year. That one season mattered more than the previous eight combined. And I want you to think about what that decision actually *is*. It's not just "we're going in a different direction" corporate-speak. It's the organizational equivalent of looking at a decade of evidence and deciding the last twelve months are more real than everything that came before.

A coach who oversaw genuine, gradual organizational improvement across several seasons can get dismissed after one disappointing recent stretch that reflects, on closer examination, an unlucky injury cascade or brutal schedule rather than any decline in the coach's own performance.

It's a decision made substantially on the strength of whichever data happened to be most recently and vividly available when someone had to make the call.

Think about what it's like to be Lovie Smith in that moment. You've spent nine years building a program. You took a team to the Super Bowl. You've won more games than you've lost. And you're being evaluated almost entirely on the basis of twelve months that happened to be the most recent twelve months, as if the previous ninety-six don't count for anything because they're further back in memory.

The message that sends to every other coach in the league is clear: your track record matters less than your last season. Your long-term results matter less than the short-term noise. The full distribution of your performance across years matters less than whichever sample happens to be most vivid when the decision gets made.

There's a dynamic here specific to how recency bias interacts with sports organizations' public-facing incentives, and it's worth naming clearly because it shows up in other domains too. Ticket sales, sponsorship revenue, media attention—all of it responds to a team's recent performance far more than to longer-run underlying quality.

A team on a hot streak sells more tickets and generates more media coverage than an equally talented team, by any fuller measure, that hasn't recently been on a comparable run.

Which means an organization's recency-driven contract and roster decisions aren't purely cognitive error. They're, in part, rational response to a recency-driven fan base and media environment that will reward the organization, in the short term, for chasing the same recent peak the statistics say is unlikely to last.

An executive who resists overpaying for a walk-year performance may be making the statistically sound decision while simultaneously making the commercially costly one, at least in the near term, because the fans and media the organization depends on for revenue are subject to the same recency bias and reward the organization for indulging it rather than correcting for it.

That creates a self-reinforcing loop. The fans overweight recent performance. The media amplifies it. The organization responds to both by making decisions that favor recent evidence. Those decisions get rewarded in ticket sales and coverage. Which teaches the organization that the recency-biased decision was the right call, at least by the metrics they're evaluated on in the short run.

The fact that those decisions systematically fail in the long run—that the walk-year contracts turn into albatrosses, that the coaches fired after one bad season go on to succeed elsewhere—doesn't register with the same force because by the time the long run arrives, everyone's moved on to the next decision, the next crisis, the next recent stretch of vivid performance that feels more real than all the data that came before it.

So what do you actually do about this?

Not as a sports franchise—you're probably not running one, and if you are, you've got consultants for this—but as a person making decisions in your own life where the same pattern shows up.

Start by writing down your baseline before the recent evidence arrives. If you're evaluating someone's performance, write down your assessment of their typical level based on everything you've seen up to now before you look at their most recent work. If you're considering a major commitment based on recent results—a hire, a partnership, a significant resource allocation—write down what you'd expect their performance to be going forward if you were basing it purely on their longer-track record, before you factor in whatever just happened.

You're not locked into that baseline. You're allowed to update it. But you're requiring yourself to notice when you do, and to articulate why this recent stretch is genuinely informative rather than just vivid.

Second, build in a waiting period between impressive recent performance and any major decision based on that performance. Not a long one—most of us don't have the luxury of waiting years. But long enough that the vividness fades slightly and you can see whether the pattern holds.

If someone does exceptional work in the month before you're deciding whether to promote them, wait another month if you can. See if it continues. If it does, you've got stronger evidence that this is a genuine shift rather than variance. If it doesn't, you've saved yourself from the equivalent of a walk-year contract.

Third—and this is the one that's hardest but matters most—build a formal override process for yourself the way the analytically sophisticated front offices do. When you're tempted to make a significant decision based primarily on recent evidence, write down the decision you'd make based on the full baseline. Then write down the decision you're actually making. If they're different, write a short note to yourself explaining why you're departing from the baseline.

You don't have to follow the baseline. Just make the departure visible.

Most of the time, the act of having to articulate the justification will reveal whether you've got genuine evidence for an update or you're just chasing recency. And the times when you override anyway—when you go with the recent evidence despite thin justification—you'll have a record of it. Which means the next time you're in a similar situation, you'll know whether your overrides tend to work out or whether they're systematically biased.

You're building your own track record on the meta-level decision: when should I trust recent evidence over the baseline, and when shouldn't I?

That record is the only thing that will actually teach you to calibrate this correctly over time, because the bias itself isn't going away. Recent evidence will always feel more real than baseline distributions. The vividness will always win the automatic, intuitive judgment.

What you're building is not a way to eliminate the bias. You're building a process that doesn't require you to eliminate it—a process that works even when the bias is still sitting there in your head, pulling your judgment toward whatever happened most recently.

The organizations that do this well aren't populated by people who are magically immune to recency bias. They're populated by people who've built systems that route around their own bias without requiring them to stop experiencing it.

And here's the thing that almost nobody says out loud about those systems: they feel bad to use.

It feels wrong to discount someone's impressive recent performance in favor of their duller baseline. It feels like you're being unfair, like you're ignoring evidence that's right in front of you, like you're letting some abstract statistical principle override the concrete reality of what you just watched happen.

That feeling doesn't mean you're wrong. It means you're doing it right.

The pull you feel toward trusting the recent evidence isn't evidence that the recent evidence is trustworthy. It's evidence that your brain works the same way everyone's does, weighting vividness over representativeness, availability over base rates, the story that just happened over the distribution that's been true all along.

When you build a process that routes around that pull, the pull doesn't go away. You just stop letting it make your decisions for you.

Which brings us to the question this chapter's been building toward, the one you probably saw coming if you've been reading closely: if we're this bad at distinguishing signal from noise in recent performance, and if the bias toward trusting recent evidence is this hard to correct even when we know it's there, what happens when the recent evidence isn't just one person's career year or one team's hot streak, but an entire market moving in one direction long enough that it starts to feel like the direction markets go?

What happens when the career year is the economy's, and the contract we're about to sign is priced in assets that just had their best run in a generation?

The Angels cap didn't fit right because they weren't buying a player—they were buying a memory of one season.

The Angels cap didn't fit right. It never would.

Chapter 5: Chasing the Last Print

On March 23, 2021, Jerome Powell used one word to describe inflation that was then running at 2.6 percent and accelerating: 'transitory.' By November, inflation hit 6.8 percent. That single word—delivered with the institutional authority of the Federal Reserve behind it—would become one of the most expensive one-word forecasts in modern central banking history.

"Transitory."

Not "concerning." Not "uncertain." Not "we're watching this closely and will adjust as needed." Transitory. The inflation numbers—then running at 2.6 percent year-over-year and accelerating month by month—would prove temporary. Supply chain disruptions from the pandemic. People returning to work. The economy shaking off Covid-era distortions. Nothing durable. Nothing requiring aggressive policy action. The Fed's formal projections, released that same week, showed inflation returning to the central bank's 2 percent target by 2022. Powell didn't hedge. Neither did the seventeen other Federal Open Market Committee members who signed off on those projections.

One year later, inflation hit 8.5 percent. By June 2022: 9.1 percent. The highest reading in forty years. The kind of number that shows up in history books, not routine quarterly reviews.

Powell is not careless. He didn't rise to chair the Federal Reserve by making lazy forecasts or ignoring evidence. Neither were the hundreds of PhD economists staffing the Federal Reserve system's research divisions—people who'd spent entire careers studying inflation dynamics, who knew the academic literature on monetary policy lags backward and forward, who had direct access to every historical parallel the data could offer. These are people trained specifically to avoid exactly the kind of mistake this chapter is about to examine.

And yet the Fed's forecast moved, month after month through 2021, in lockstep with whatever the most recent Consumer Price Index release showed. When a monthly print ran cool in April, the projections barely budged. When one ran hot in May, they revised up—but always anchored to what had *just happened*, extrapolating the freshest number forward rather than treating it as one noisy observation inside a rapidly shifting regime.

I know what you're thinking. The Fed just got unlucky. They were working with incomplete information, making real-time judgments under uncertainty, and the economy threw them a curveball nobody could have called. And look—that's partly true. Economic forecasting is genuinely hard. The future is unknowable in ways that make predicting it, with precision, impossible for anyone.

But that's not quite what happened here.

Economic forecasting occupies a strange position among the domains this book has examined so far. Unlike political punditry, where the resolution date sits years out and memory fades, economic forecasts resolve *fast*. A GDP projection made in January gets graded against reality by April. An inflation forecast has a shelf life measured in months, not election cycles. You don't get to hide behind ambiguity or wait for everyone to forget what you said. The number either shows up or it doesn't.

And the people making these forecasts—the trained economists at central banks, investment banks, consulting firms, government agencies—have direct access to the same historical data, the same models, the same academic papers documenting exactly how badly forecasters tend to do when they extrapolate recent trends. If recency bias were primarily a knowledge problem, fixable by reading the right studies or sitting through the right training session, professional economic forecasters should be the population *least* vulnerable to it.

They're not. They're one of the populations where it shows up most cleanly.

—

In early 2006, I bought into a Denver rental property investment with a neighbor who'd made 40 percent on two flips in the previous eighteen months. His pitch arrived on a Saturday afternoon—I remember the setting because it felt casual, unthreatening, the kind of conversation that happens over a backyard fence rather than in a broker's office. He brought a printout. Recent sales comps from the neighborhood, highlighted in yellow. Every property selling for more than the last one. Every month higher than the month before. The chart didn't just trend upward—it accelerated upward, each data point pulling away from the previous one with the kind of momentum that makes extrapolation feel less like speculation and more like simple arithmetic.

We didn't think we were being reckless. We thought we were responding to *data*. And we were—we were responding to the most recent data, which happened to be the least informative part of the data available to us, if we'd known how to weight it properly.

I put down $85,000.

Three years of price increases, dramatic as they felt, were a short window inside a much longer housing market history that included multiple periods where prices went sideways or fell. I just didn't weight that history the same way I weighted what had happened in the last eighteen months. The recent comps were vivid. Fresh. Right there on the page in front of me. The longer trend required effort to reconstruct—digging through county records, calling real estate agents who'd worked the area in the nineties, piecing together a picture that wasn't nearly as clean or immediate as the printout showing six quarters of uninterrupted gains.

By 2009, the property was worth less than my down payment.

I'd mistaken three years of momentum for a permanently new reality. The same mistake Jerome Powell made in 2021. The same mistake professional forecasters make quarter after quarter in ways the research literature has documented in painful detail. The only difference is scale. My mistake cost me $85,000 and a friendship with the neighbor I stopped making eye contact with after the foreclosure. The Fed's cost the economy years of elevated inflation and the most aggressive rate-hiking cycle in four decades.

—

Researchers studying how professional forecasters revise their published expectations have an unusual advantage over people studying, say, how voters form opinions or how juries weigh evidence. The economic forecasting world generates survey data—lots of it—that tracks the same individual forecasters over time, letting you see exactly how a specific person's prediction changes from one period to the next in response to newly released information. You can measure, with precision, whether the revision someone made was proportional to the actual new information that arrived, or whether they moved too far.

The pattern that emerges, replicated across multiple studies and multiple countries, has a technical name in the academic literature:

extrapolative expectation formation. The plain-language version is simpler, and more damning.

Forecasters revise their expectations by *more* than the new information justifies, in the direction of whatever the most recent data release showed. Then, when the extrapolation overshoots—when the thing they just revised toward doesn't continue—they have to revise back.

This isn't a fringe finding from one questionable study. It's one of the sturdier, more frequently replicated results in behavioral macroeconomics. And it's harder to dismiss than findings about, say, retail investors buying Bitcoin at the peak or sports bettors chasing last week's upset winner, precisely because the population being studied consists of people whose entire professional training was designed to prevent exactly this mistake.

The mechanism doesn't require assuming incompetence. A quarterly data release—an inflation number, an employment report, a revised GDP estimate—arrives as a single, crisp, freshly available figure. It's a *number*. Clean. Precise. Definitive. It lands on your desk (or your screen) on a fixed schedule, accompanied by a Bureau of Labor Statistics press release and a flood of financial media coverage analyzing what it means. The number is *vivid*. Immediate. You don't have to reconstruct it from memory or dig through old spreadsheets to find it. It's right there, demanding attention, at the exact moment you need to update your forecast.

The longer underlying trend—the one that number is either confirming or deviating from—is an abstraction by comparison. It's still there. Still true. But reconstructing it requires effort. You have to pull up a chart, scroll back through the data, remind yourself what the pattern looked like before this newest release arrived.

The recent number has the same structural advantage the last witness had in Chapter 3's courtroom: it sits in front of you, vivid and immediate, at the exact moment judgment has to be rendered. The full historical record competes at a disadvantage, regardless of how much more informative it actually is.

—

Picture an analyst at a mid-sized investment bank—call her Sarah, senior economist, responsible for maintaining the firm's multi-year economic outlook that gets distributed to institutional clients every quarter. The outlook has tracked a moderate growth trajectory for several quarters. Nothing flashy. Nothing alarming. Just steady 2-to-3 percent GDP growth quarter after quarter, the kind of stable expansion that makes for boring commentary but reliable forecasting. Each individual release has landed close enough to that trend that no major revision seemed warranted. Sarah's job, most months, is repetitive in the way that builds confidence. Update the spreadsheet. Confirm the trend still holds. Send the revised deck to clients. Repeat.

Then the Bureau of Economic Analysis drops a surprise. Third-quarter GDP growth comes in at 4.2 percent annualized—well above Sarah's forecast, well above consensus, well above the 2.5 percent average the economy's been tracking for two years.

What should a rational forecaster do with this?

Some revision makes sense. Obviously. A single surprising data point *does* carry information. The question isn't whether to update—it's how much weight that one new observation should get relative to the longer trend. If you're doing this formally, the way economists are trained to do it, you'd use something called Bayesian updating. You'd weigh the new observation against your forecast's existing precision. A well-established trend built on many quarters of consistent data should move only modestly in response to one new, noisy observation. The single data point gets counted for what it is: a small increment of new evidence against a multi-year base, not a wholesale replacement of everything you knew before it arrived.

What actually happens—documented across years of forecaster surveys—is a revision considerably larger than that.

The single surprising quarter gets treated as though it were nearly as informative as the entire trend it's deviating from. Sarah bumps the full-year growth outlook up by half a percentage point, maybe more. The revision shows up in the next client deck as a "strengthening growth picture," illustrated with a chart where the recent quarter sits at the right edge, visually dominating everything that came before it.

Not because Sarah sat down and consciously decided, "I'm going to ignore two years of data and extrapolate from one quarter." That's not how it feels from the inside. It feels like responding appropriately to new information. The 4.2 percent number is *fresh*. It's what every client email and every morning meeting and every CNBC segment has been talking about since Thursday when the release hit. The two-year trend is still there in the spreadsheet, still true, but it requires deliberate effort to keep it front-of-mind in a way the newest number doesn't.

The revised outlook moves toward the strong quarter by more than the statistics justify. Not because Sarah abandoned the multi-year trend as stated methodology, but because the single quarter got to count, in practice, for more than one data point's worth of evidence.

Here's where it compounds. Sarah doesn't work in isolation. She reads other forecasters' reports. She watches market prices—equity indexes, bond yields, commodity futures—that are themselves responding to the same data release, often in exaggerated ways that make the "surprising" number look even more significant. She reads financial media coverage that has, by its own structural incentives, strong reasons to treat every new release as more meaningful than "broadly consistent with the existing trend" would sound.

Bloomberg doesn't run headlines saying, "Third Quarter GDP Confirms What We Already Knew." CNBC doesn't book guests to discuss continuity. The media apparatus surrounding economic forecasting has its own built-in amplifier for exactly the kind of extrapolative reading the underlying cognitive bias already predisposes forecasters toward.

The result—visible across years of financial commentary if you bother to go back and read it in sequence—is a public conversation about the economy's direction that whipsaws between competing narratives with a frequency the actual underlying data rarely justifies.

A run of stronger-than-expected releases in late 2017 and early 2018 produced declarations that durable acceleration had arrived. That 3 percent trend growth was back. That the Federal Reserve was "behind the curve" and needed to raise rates faster to keep up. Larry Kudlow, then the new director of the National Economic Council, went on Fox Business in April 2018 and called it "an economic boom." Final GDP growth for 2018: 2.5 percent. Exactly in line with the pre-2018 trend. The boom was a mirage created by extrapolating three strong quarters.

A subsequent run of weaker data through 2019 produced an equally confident wave of recession warnings. The New York Fed's recession probability model hit 38 percent. The Treasury yield curve inverted—a classic recession signal that got covered as though the downturn were already inevitable, already baked in, just waiting for the calendar to catch up to what the bond market already knew. No recession arrived. The economy kept growing at roughly the same moderate pace it had been growing at all along, before either narrative took hold.

Viewed individually, each round of commentary was responding to real, accurately reported data. Viewed in sequence, the pattern looks less like independent reassessments and more like a stable trend being narrated, over and over, as a series of regime changes. Each new data point treated as the one *finally* revealing the true direction, until the next data point reveals a different direction, in a cycle that repeats without the underlying reality having moved nearly as much as the narrative implied it did.

—

You might be thinking this is just professional incentives at work, not cognitive bias. That forecasters extrapolate because it's *safer* to be wrong with the herd than to be right alone. And you'd be partly correct. There's a real career-risk dimension here that makes the pattern worse.

A forecaster whose published expectations track close to consensus faces relatively little professional danger even when consensus turns out catastrophically wrong. Being wrong with everyone else—getting "transitory" wrong alongside Jerome Powell and every major Wall Street economist—rarely damages an individual reputation the way being wrong *alone* does. When the entire profession misses the same turning point, it gets filed under "inherent uncertainty" rather than "professional failure." Nobody loses their job for matching consensus. You can build an entire decades-long career as a well-compensated economist without ever making a forecast that deviates meaningfully from the median view, simply by being a competent trend-extrapolator with good timing.

A forecaster who resists extrapolating from a single surprising release, who holds to a longer-horizon view the full historical record would support, takes on different risk. If the longer view turns out right, the reward is muted. "I said the trend would hold" doesn't generate the same attention as "I called the turn." It doesn't get you booked on CNBC or quoted in the Wall Street Journal or invited to present at the big industry conferences. If it's wrong—or even if it's right on a timescale longer than clients are willing to wait for—the forecaster bears that cost alone, without the cover of having moved with the herd.

This asymmetry gives individually rational forecasters a professional incentive to extrapolate even in cases where their private judgment, unconstrained by career concerns, might lean toward treating the surprise as noise.

But incentives and cognition aren't separate forces here. They're reinforcing each other. The recency bias makes the extrapolative forecast *feel* justified—it doesn't feel like you're abandoning two years of data, it feels like you're incorporating important new information. The professional incentives then reward exactly that feeling, making it financially safer to go with what the bias was already pushing you toward anyway.

The result is a forecasting environment where the people most qualified to resist recency bias have the weakest incentive structure supporting that resistance.

—

Let me tell you what it costs when this pattern runs at scale.

Not in abstract terms. Not as a theoretical inefficiency or a minor drag on forecasting accuracy that gets averaged out across many predictions. What it costs in lived, concrete, human terms when an entire profession mistakes momentum for permanence.

The Fed's "transitory" call in 2021 wasn't just wrong. It delayed the policy response by more than a year—a year in which inflation went from a manageable 2.6 percent to a crisis-level 9.1 percent. When the Fed finally did act, they had to raise rates faster and higher than would have been necessary if they'd started earlier. The federal funds rate went from near-zero to over 5 percent in less than eighteen months—the most aggressive tightening cycle since Paul Volcker's war on inflation in the early 1980s.

That speed has consequences. Real ones. Not for Jerome Powell, who still has his job and his salary and his pension. For the people whose lives got upended by what followed.

Mortgage rates doubled. The 30-year fixed rate that sat at 3 percent in early 2022 hit 7 percent by late 2023. A couple who qualified for a $400,000 mortgage at 3 percent suddenly qualified for $280,000 at 7 percent—a difference that, in many housing markets, meant the difference between buying a home and getting priced out entirely. First-time homebuyers, the population with the least financial cushion and the least ability to wait out a rate cycle, bore the brunt of this. Homeownership rates for adults under 35 dropped to the lowest level in decades.

Small business lending froze. A restaurant owner in Atlanta who'd been planning an expansion—second location, more staff, the kind of investment that comes from confidence in a stable future—watched her borrowing costs triple and shelved the plan indefinitely. Commercial real estate developers stopped breaking ground on new projects because the math no longer worked at the higher rates. Construction jobs dried up. Not because demand disappeared. Because the policy response to a forecasting error made the financing unworkable.

Corporate layoffs followed. Tech companies that had staffed up aggressively in the low-rate environment of 2020 and 2021—betting on continued expansion, on durable growth—suddenly faced a different economic reality and started cutting. Meta laid off 11,000 employees in November 2022. Amazon cut 18,000 jobs in early 2023. Google, Microsoft, Salesforce—each shedding thousands of workers in a span of months, not because the underlying business had collapsed, but because the macroeconomic environment had shifted faster than anyone had forecast.

These weren't abstractions. These were people. Software engineers who'd relocated their families for jobs that evaporated. Mid-career professionals who'd felt secure and suddenly weren't. Recent graduates entering a labor market that had tightened seemingly overnight.

And it all traces back to the same cognitive error this chapter has been circling: treating the most recent data as though it were the most informative data, when the opposite was true.

The Fed wasn't ignoring information. They were responding to it—responding too much, too confidently, to information that arrived fresh and vivid and immediate at the expense of the longer, quieter trend that should have anchored their judgment. They extrapolated from twelve months of "transitory" readings without adequately weighting the historical record showing how quickly inflationary regimes can shift once certain thresholds get crossed.

It's easy to say, in retrospect, that they should have known better. But that's the thing about recency bias. It doesn't *feel* like bias from the inside. It feels like being appropriately responsive to new information. The mistake isn't visible until you're already deep into it.

—

Economic data has a further complication that makes all this worse: the data itself gets revised.

An early estimate of quarterly GDP is typically refined, sometimes substantially, as more complete underlying data trickles in over the weeks and months following the initial release. This means the "recent data point" driving an extrapolative forecast revision is often not even a settled *fact* at the moment it's exerting maximum influence. It's a preliminary estimate, subject to change, that gets treated with the same weight a final, confirmed figure would receive—simply because it's the freshest number available when the forecast needs updating.

In July 2021, the Bureau of Economic Analysis released its initial estimate of second-quarter GDP growth: 6.5 percent annualized. Strong. Well above consensus. Well above what most forecasters had penciled in. Financial media coverage framed it as confirmation the recovery was accelerating faster than expected. Forecasters bumped their outlooks higher. Investment banks upgraded their growth projections. Market commentary shifted toward a "stronger for longer" narrative.

Two months later, the third and final revision came out. The number: 6.3 percent.

Not a huge change—0.2 percentage points—but enough to matter when you remember that people were extrapolating forward from the initial 6.5 percent figure, using it as the foundation for multi-year forecasts. They were building expectations on top of a number that would itself look different within weeks, compounding ordinary recency distortion with an additional layer of noise the forecaster had no way to detect when the extrapolation was made.

The public conversation amplifies all of this through another channel: the treatment of forecast *revisions* as newsworthy events, independent of whether the revision reflects a meaningful change in economic trajectory or just ordinary, expected noise.

A minor upward adjustment to a growth forecast—well within the normal range of quarter-to-quarter tweaking—can generate headlines framing it as confirmation of a turning point, simply because "Forecasters Raise Outlook" is more publishable than "Forecasters Make Routine Adjustment."

Readers encountering this coverage have no way to distinguish, from the headline alone, a significant revision from a routine one. The resulting narrative, built from a sequence of headlines each treating ordinary adjustment as dramatic event, ends up more volatile in its apparent implications than the underlying forecasts themselves would justify.

—

Corporate earnings forecasting shows the same pattern on a faster cycle, because companies report quarterly results on a fixed, predictable schedule. Every three months. For every publicly traded company. Across an entire market simultaneously.

A single quarter's earnings report is exactly the kind of vivid, freshly available data point this chapter's been circling: released on a known date, covered extensively within hours, immediately incorporated into analysts' revised price targets and buy/sell recommendations.

And the revisions that follow—both to earnings estimates and to stock prices—consistently overshoot what a single quarter's performance, evaluated against a multi-year track record, would rationally justify.

Companies that beat expectations tend to see price targets revised upward by amounts difficult to square with the information content of one quarter relative to a longer trajectory. Companies that disappoint see the inverse. Price targets get slashed. Ratings get downgraded. The stock sells off. All in response to a single quarter's shortfall that, viewed against the company's full history, often sits well within the normal range of quarterly variation.

Apple's July 2023 earnings offer a clean example because the "miss" was so small it should have been irrelevant. The company reported third-quarter revenue of $81.8 billion. Analyst consensus had been $81.97 billion. The miss: 0.2 percent. A rounding error. Well within the normal range of quarterly noise for a company of Apple's scale, operating across dozens of product lines and a hundred different countries, subject to currency fluctuations and seasonal variations that make any single quarter's results inherently noisy.

Over the following week, analysts cut their twelve-month price targets by an average of 3 percent—fifteen times the size of the revenue miss. Some cuts were steeper. Morgan Stanley dropped its target from $180 to $177. Bank of America went from $208 to $205. These weren't responses to new information about Apple's long-term competitive position or market opportunity. They were mechanical reactions to one quarter coming in slightly below a three-month-old estimate.

The stock dropped 6 percent in the days following the earnings call—a $150 billion decline in market capitalization triggered by a revenue shortfall of $170 million. The ratio is absurd on its face. A company doesn't lose $150 billion in durable enterprise value because one quarter's sales came in 0.2 percent below an estimate that was itself subject to all the usual forecasting error.

But the pattern repeats, quarter after quarter, across thousands of companies. Beat expectations: stock jumps, price targets rise, bullish commentary proliferates. Miss expectations: stock drops, targets fall, concerns mount about the company's trajectory. The magnitude of the reaction routinely exceeds what the information content of a single quarter would justify, if that quarter were being evaluated against the company's full history rather than against the three-month-old consensus estimate it's being compared to.

—

Some forecasting methodologies try to build structural defenses against this.

Trend-filtering techniques—statistical approaches that explicitly separate a "trend" component from a "noise" component—are designed to isolate the durable underlying pattern from single-period volatility. They function as pre-committed standards, set in advance, so no single fresh release can retroactively rewrite the rule being used to interpret it.

They don't *prevent* a forecaster from overriding the filtered estimate. Nothing prevents that, any more than a valuation model prevents an executive from overpaying for an acquisition anyway. But building the conservative, full-record-weighted estimate as the visible *default*—requiring an explicit, justified departure rather than treating extrapolation as the unmarked response to new information—shifts the burden of proof in the direction the underlying statistics warrant.

The question is whether you're willing to use them. Whether you're willing to build a forecast where the recent surprising data point gets the weight it statistically deserves—which is often much less than it *feels* like it deserves—rather than letting recency do its usual work.

That choice has asymmetric consequences. Get it right, and you avoid the whipsaw. You don't chase the last print into territory the full record wouldn't support. You don't have to revise back when the surprise turns out to be noise. You don't mistake three years of momentum for a permanently new reality.

Get it wrong—extrapolate when you should have held the trend—and you bear the cost alone. No cover from consensus. No "everyone missed it" defense. Just you, holding a forecast the recent data has already moved past, waiting to see whether the longer record vindicates you or whether you should have chased the momentum after all.

Most forecasters, faced with that asymmetry, chase. It's individually rational even when it's collectively destructive. Even when it produces exactly the kind of systematic error the research literature has documented across decades of professional forecasting.

—

Here's what you do with this.

First: when you encounter a forecast—economic, corporate, political, personal—that's been recently revised in the direction of whatever surprising new information just arrived, ask what fraction of the total evidence that new information actually represents.

One strong quarter against two years of moderate growth is one data point against eight. One month's inflation reading against a year of prior readings is one observation against twelve. The revision should be proportional to that ratio, not to how surprising or vivid or heavily covered the recent release was.

If the revision is larger than the statistical weight would justify, you're watching extrapolation, not updating. And extrapolation, as a betting strategy, has a well-documented track record. It wins while momentum continues. It loses, badly, when momentum breaks.

Second: build your own trend estimate before the surprising data arrives, and commit to it in writing. Not as a rigid forecast you'll never update, but as a baseline against which to measure how much any single new observation should move you.

The problem isn't updating. The problem is updating by too much, in a way you can't see clearly when the fresh data is sitting right in front of you demanding attention. Having a pre-committed trend estimate—something you wrote down before the surprise arrived—gives you a reference point that isn't contaminated by the vividness of whatever just happened.

Third: if you're responsible for making forecasts professionally—if you're the economist at the investment bank, the analyst covering earnings, the executive projecting next year's budget—build structural constraints that prevent any single data release from moving your forecast by more than the statistics justify.

Trend filters. Multi-year averages. Bayesian updating rules that explicitly weight new observations against your existing base of evidence. Whatever form it takes, the goal is the same: make extrapolation *hard*. Make it require a deliberate, justified override rather than being the default response to new information.

The forecasters who do this aren't trying to be contrarian. They're trying to be *proportional*. To give each piece of evidence the weight it deserves based on its information content, not based on how recently it arrived or how much media coverage it generated or how many other forecasters have already revised toward it.

Fourth: when you're evaluating someone else's forecast, look at the *sequence* of revisions, not just the current estimate. A forecast that whipsaws—revising up after strong data, then down after weak data, then up again—is revealing something about its methodology. It's telling you the forecaster is extrapolating from recent releases rather than holding to a longer trend.

That doesn't mean the current forecast is wrong. But it does mean the forecast is systematically vulnerable to exactly the error this chapter has been examining, which should adjust how much confidence you place in it.

Fifth, and most important: resist the feeling that recent data is *more real* than older data.

This is the core of the bias. Not that recent information is worthless—it's not. But that it *feels* more informative than it actually is, simply because it's fresh and vivid and sitting right in front of you at the moment judgment needs to be rendered.

The two-year trend is just as real as this quarter's surprise. The ten-year average is just as factual as this month's release. They're harder to keep in mind. They require deliberate effort to reconstruct. They don't get headlines or CNBC segments or breathless commentary about what they *mean*.

But they're real. And in most cases—not all, but most—they're more informative than whatever just happened, simply because they represent more observations, more variation, more opportunities for the underlying pattern to reveal itself against the noise.

The forecasters who've built careers on getting this right aren't smarter than their extrapolating peers. They're not working with better data or more sophisticated models. They've just found ways to resist the gravitational pull of recency—to weight the full record more heavily than the single vivid number that arrived this morning—in an environment where every incentive pushes the other direction.

That resistance is learnable. It's a skill, not a personality trait. But it requires building systems that do the work for you, because willpower alone won't be enough when the fresh data lands and every colleague and every headline and every market price is telling you the trend just changed.

—

The pattern this chapter has traced—from Powell's "transitory" to my Denver rental to Sarah's GDP revision to Apple's earnings miss—isn't a story about forecasting error. It's a story about what happens when we mistake momentum for truth.

Not because we're careless. Because momentum is the only pattern we can see clearly in the moment. It's vivid. Immediate. Undeniable. The chart goes up, month after month, and extrapolating from that feels less like speculation and more like reading what's already written.

Until it stops. And by then you're holding a forecast—or a property, or a position, or a budget—that was never grounded in anything more durable than the last few prints.

The full record was always there. You just had to want to see it more than you wanted to believe the recent trend would continue. Most of us don't. Not because we can't, but because the incentives and the cognition and the media environment and the career pressures all push the same direction, and swimming against that current requires more than good intentions.

It requires systems. Defaults. Pre-committed rules that prevent the fresh data from counting for more than it should, simply because it's fresh.

The question isn't whether you'll face this choice. You will. The next time a surprising data release lands, the next time a recent trend looks like it's revealing something durable, the next time momentum builds and everyone around you starts extrapolating—you'll face the same choice Sarah faced, the same choice Powell faced, the same choice I faced looking at that printout of Denver comps in 2006.

The question is whether you'll have built the systems, in advance, that let you give the surprising number the weight it deserves—and no more—rather than the weight it feels like it deserves when it's sitting right in front of you, demanding to be believed.

The hardest part isn't recognizing the trap after you've fallen into it. By then the damage is done—the position is on, the property is under contract, the capital is committed. The hardest part is recognizing the trap *before* you're in it, when the data still looks like signal and not yet like noise, when the story still feels like insight and not yet like rationalization.

Here's what makes it harder: the last print *might* be right. The trend *might* be turning. The surprising number *might* be the first visible crack in a structure that's about to collapse, or the first visible proof of a shift that's about to dominate. Dismissing it entirely is just as dangerous as embracing it entirely. The goal isn't to ignore recency. The goal is to *contextualize* it—to give it the weight it deserves within the full distribution of evidence, rather than letting it hijack the entire decision.

That requires building what I think of as *temporal diversification* into your data diet. Not just looking at different asset classes or different markets, but looking at different *time windows* simultaneously, so that no single window—especially not the most recent one—can dominate your perception of what's true.

In practice, that means asking, every time a new number lands: *What would I believe if I hadn't seen this number yet?* Not as a way to dismiss the number, but as a way to establish a prior—a baseline view of the world that existed before this particular data point arrived. Then you can ask: *How much does this number move me off that prior?* A little? A lot? Entirely?

If the answer is "entirely," you're almost certainly overreacting. A single print, no matter how surprising, rarely contains enough information to overturn an entire framework built on months or years of accumulated evidence. It might *update* that framework. It might shift probabilities at the margin. But it shouldn't collapse the whole structure.

I learned this the expensive way. After Denver, I spent years trying to insulate myself from recency bias by building rigid rules—never act on data less than three months old, never extrapolate from a single quarter, never trust a trend until it's survived at least two policy cycles. The rules helped, but they also made me slow. I missed entries I should have taken. I dismissed early signals that turned out to be correct. I mistook rigidity for discipline.

What I needed wasn't *more* rules. What I needed was a framework that let me integrate new information without being dominated by it—a way to update my beliefs in real time without letting the most recent observation erase everything I'd learned before it.

Bayesian updating is the formal version of this. You start with a prior probability—your best guess about the state of the world before seeing new evidence. Then, when new evidence arrives, you update that probability in proportion to how surprising the evidence is *given* your prior. If the evidence is highly unexpected under your current model, it moves you a lot. If it's roughly consistent with what you already believed, it moves you a little.

The beauty of this approach is that it doesn't require you to ignore recency. It just requires you to *weight* recency appropriately—to let the new data speak, but not shout over everything else you know.

But here's the problem: most of us don't walk around with explicit priors. We don't have a number in our heads representing our pre-existing belief about cap rates or absorption or where the Fed is headed. We have a vague sense, a feeling, a collection of half-formed intuitions. And when a sharp, clear, recent number arrives, it overwhelms the vague. The concrete beats the fuzzy, even when the fuzzy is built on years of accumulated pattern recognition and the concrete is built on one data point.

So the real work isn't mathematical. It's operational. It's building systems that *force* you to articulate your prior before the new data arrives, so that when the new data lands, you have something solid to anchor against.

For me, that means writing down my base case. Not elaborate models—just a simple, declarative summary of what I believe is most likely to happen over the next six to twelve months, and why. I update it quarterly, not in response to news, which means it captures what I believe when I'm *not* reacting to the latest print. Then, when something surprising happens, I have a written record of what I thought before I saw it. I can compare. I can ask: *Does this change my base case, or does it just add noise?* And I can update deliberately, rather than reflexively.

It's not foolproof. There are still moments when a single number feels so significant, so clarifying, that it's hard not to let it rewrite everything. But having the prior written down makes it harder to pretend I didn't have one. It makes it harder to let the new data sneak in and occupy the entire frame.

The other thing that helps is remembering that recency bias doesn't just show up in how you interpret data. It shows up in *which* data you choose to look at. When you're already leaning in a particular direction—already inclined to believe that the market is turning, or that a trend is accelerating—you start seeking out the numbers that confirm that inclination. And because the most recent numbers are the easiest to find, the easiest to cite, the easiest to hang a narrative on, they're the ones you reach for.

You don't do this consciously. You do it because the human brain is wired to resolve ambiguity, to find coherence, to turn a cloud of conflicting signals into a single story. And the most recent signal is always the easiest thread to pull.

That's why I force myself to look backward before I look forward. Before I check this month's data, I re-read last quarter's. Before I react to the latest report, I pull up the same report from a year ago, two years ago, five years ago. Not to dismiss the present, but to remind myself that the present is one frame in a much longer film—and that every previous frame felt just as urgent, just as definitive, as this one does now.

None of this makes you immune. You'll still overweight the recent. You'll still get pulled toward the last print. But you'll catch yourself faster. You'll notice the tilt before you've committed. And over time, you'll build the reflex that matters most: the reflex to ask, before you act on any piece of new information, *What am I forgetting?*

Because the answer is always something. The answer is always that there's a longer pattern, a deeper context, a base rate that the recent number is either consistent with or deviating from—and you won't know which until you look.

The last print is never the whole story. But it's always the loudest. And if you let it, it will be the only story you hear.

One word—transitory—condensed eighteen months of evidence into a forecast anchored to the most recent print.

'Transitory' was the word Powell chose. By November, inflation hit 6.8 percent.

Chapter 6: The Debate That Decided Nothing

The cameras were live. October 6, 1976, Walnut Street Theater in Philadelphia. President Gerald Ford stood at his podium across from Jimmy Carter, under lights so hot both men's makeup needed touch-ups between segments.

Max Frankel of the New York Times rose to ask about Soviet influence in Eastern Europe. Standard foreign policy territory. The kind of question Ford had fielded hundreds of times.

Ford's answer came quickly. "There is no Soviet domination of Eastern Europe, and there never will be under a Ford administration."

The room went quiet. Not the respectful quiet that follows a strong answer. The other kind.

Frankel looked genuinely surprised—you can see it in the footage. He did something reporters almost never do in that setting. He offered Ford a lifeline. A follow-up question. Space to clarify. Ford didn't take it. He doubled down. Insisted the Yugoslavians, the Romanians, the Poles didn't consider themselves dominated by Moscow.

The camera cuts to his advisors. One of them closes his eyes. Another's mouth is open.

Over the next three weeks, that ninety-second exchange became the entire race. Not Ford's record as president. Not the economy. Not hundreds of policy positions articulated across months of campaigning. One moment. Replayed on every evening newscast, dissected in every major newspaper, treated as the thing that explained everything you needed to know about why Gerald Ford wasn't fit to be president.

Ford lost three weeks later. Two percentage points.

The question isn't whether Ford's answer was bad. It was.

The question is whether that ninety-second exchange actually deserved the explanatory weight it got handed—both in real time and in every retrospective analysis that followed. Whether it could really tell voters more about Ford's fitness for office than everything else in his three-year record combined.

Or whether it mattered mostly because it happened last.

I've watched this pattern my whole adult life. Campaign professionals know—at a level so deep they don't even think about it anymore—that timing shapes everything. That's why ad spending concentrates so heavily in the closing stretch. Why message discipline tightens as election day approaches. Why campaigns obsess over "controlling the narrative" in that final sprint.

Everyone inside the profession understands that events closer to the vote exert more influence than events of equal substance that occurred earlier.

But no one wants to say it out loud that way. Because saying it out loud would mean admitting we don't actually weigh evidence the way we think we do.

The pattern shows up everywhere. Every contested race produces its own version of "the moment that decided everything." A debate stumble. A hot mic. A last-minute endorsement. A final-week scandal. The specifics change every cycle. The structure never does.

Here's a scene I keep coming back to.

Picture two people watching the same late-campaign disaster unfold. Same building, same day. One is a senior strategist for the candidate whose moment just went badly. The other is a political columnist covering the race.

The strategist, in an emergency staff meeting, argues the damage is temporary. A media fixation. She urges her team not to amplify the story by responding—let it fade. She's confident voters will weigh the full record when they actually cast their ballots.

The columnist, writing under deadline two floors down, frames the same event completely differently. He treats it as revelatory. A window into who this candidate really is beneath all the carefully managed messaging. Evidence of a deeper character flaw the electorate simply hadn't noticed until now.

Both people saw the same thing happen. Both are constructing entirely different narratives about what it means.

And both are making the same underlying mistake.

They're granting a single recent event diagnostic weight that has nothing to do with its actual size relative to everything else that's happened. One does it defensively. The other does it offensively. But both are overweighting the recent data point, using it to rewrite the fuller story they should be telling instead.

This isn't just human error. The institution reinforces it.

A news cycle rewards novelty. "The race remains fundamentally unchanged" isn't a publishable headline. "This moment changes everything" reliably generates clicks, shares, engagement—the metrics that determine whether political coverage survives financially. So there's structural pressure, built into the business model of political journalism itself, to treat each new campaign event as more significant than a dispassionate accounting of the full record would support.

The institution can't afford not to.

Which creates a kind of collaboration between our cognitive bias and the economic incentives of the media covering the thing we're trying to assess. The bias wants to treat the recent thing as more important. The business model needs to treat the recent thing as more important. They lock together. And pretty soon you're living in a shared reality where the recent event doesn't just *feel* more important—it *becomes* more important, because everyone's treating it that way, because the narrative around it has crowded out everything else so thoroughly that trying to point to the fuller record makes you sound like you're making excuses or hopelessly out of touch.

Let me be specific about what this costs us.

When Ford lost that election, the dominant explanation became "the debate." The Eastern Europe answer. That's what people remembered. That's what got cited in every election post-mortem. That's what went into the history books as the turning point.

But political scientists who've actually studied the 1976 race have found something more modest. The underlying determinants of that election—the economy, partisan identification, fundamentals established well before the final weeks—explained more of the outcome than any single closing event, however dramatic it looked.

Ford was already in trouble before that debate. The economy had been rough—inflation, unemployment, the hangover from the 1973 oil crisis. He'd inherited a presidency damaged by Watergate and never been elected to it himself. He'd pardoned Nixon. The fundamentals weren't in his favor.

The debate exchange probably moved the margin somewhat. But treating it as *the* explanation for why Ford lost requires ignoring a lot of other things that mattered more—things that had been in place for months, but weren't as vivid, weren't as recent, didn't make for as clean a story.

Think about what that means.

We took a complex election shaped by multiple factors accumulated over years, and we compressed it into a single ninety-second moment because that moment was fresh and dramatic and easy to remember. We built a whole explanation around it. We taught that explanation to the next generation of campaign professionals, who learned the wrong lesson—not "don't make factual errors in debates" (though that's not a bad lesson), but "the last thing that happens is the thing that explains everything," which is just recency bias wearing a graduate degree.

And here's the thing—you probably already know this, at some level. If I asked you right now whether a single debate exchange should outweigh three years of presidential performance, you'd say no. Of course not.

But when the exchange is fresh, when it's playing on every screen, when every conversation you overhear is about it, when the columnist you respect is writing that it "reveals who this candidate really is"—in that moment, the recent thing doesn't feel like we're overweighting it.

It feels real. It feels like new information that genuinely changes what we know.

That's the trap. We don't believe recent data is predictive. We believe it's *real*. Which feels completely different but produces exactly the same error.

There's an asymmetry here worth naming.

Campaign staff live inside a higher-frequency information stream than anyone observing from outside. Polling data. Focus groups. Message testing. Tracking polls that update daily, sometimes twice daily in competitive races. They're exposed to fresh evidence constantly.

Which doesn't train them out of overweighting recent information—it just supplies the bias with more frequent material to seize on.

I talked to someone who worked on a Senate race a few cycles back. He described what it's like inside that environment during the final month. The campaign gets a tracking poll every evening. Every evening, the number moves. Up two points. Down three points. Up one point. Every evening, there's a meeting where people who absolutely should know better treat that movement as meaningful. As actionable. As requiring a strategic response.

"You know rationally it's noise," he told me. "You know most day-to-day movement in a tracking poll is just statistical variation around a stable trend. Sample error. You've read the methodology section. You understand confidence intervals. But you're in the room, and everyone's looking at the number, and the candidate is looking at you, and someone's asking 'what are we going to do about this,' and the pressure to react—to do *something*—is enormous."

He described watching his own campaign reverse a strategic decision they'd made two weeks earlier based on focus group research, because the tracking poll moved three points in the wrong direction over forty-eight hours. They changed their closing message. Pulled ads. Cut new ones.

The tracking poll bounced back four days later.

The new ads were already running.

A campaign that had done the hard work of understanding its electorate—that had invested in focus groups, that had built a message around what those groups revealed, that had committed to a strategy weeks in advance—abandoned all of it because a single data point moved in an unexpected direction.

Not because the new data was better than the old data. But because the tracking poll was *recent*, and recent data hijacks our assessment of what's true even when we know better.

A campaign that reacts to every tracking-poll fluctuation as meaningful signal ends up whipsawing. Lurching from crisis mode to confidence and back again. Reversing strategy in response to fluctuations that, examined against the full polling record, mostly cancel out.

You know what that feels like inside a campaign? Exhausting. Disorienting. Like you're steering a ship through fog where the compass spins every time you look at it.

The people I've talked to who survived with their sanity intact all describe the same thing: at some point they had to build a deliberate defense against their own instinct to react to every new piece of information as though it rewrote everything they knew. The ones who didn't build that defense burned out, or made catastrophic strategic errors, or both.

Some campaigns have figured this out. Some of the more methodologically careful operations that analyze elections from outside have too.

FiveThirtyEight—before Nate Silver left—built polling aggregation models that combined many individual polls into a single trend-weighted estimate rather than reacting to any one poll's release. The Economist's election model does something similar. They're doing the same thing trend-filtering does for economic data. Building, in advance, a standard that discounts single-point noise relative to accumulated evidence.

No single poll, no single news cycle, gets to retroactively rewrite the standard.

Some campaigns have adopted comparable internal discipline. They commit to a core narrative built around the race's fundamentals well before the final weeks, specifically so they won't reactively rebuild their entire strategy around whatever event happened most recently. They decide, in July, what story they're telling about the race. Then they stick to it through October even when the pressure to pivot is overwhelming.

This carries real professional cost. When everyone else in the political conversation is treating a moment as decisive, declining to react visibly takes nerve. You look out of touch. You look like you're not taking the crisis seriously. You look like you're losing.

But it works the same way the sports front office's pre-committed valuation model works: by locking in the standard before the late data arrives, you protect yourself from getting hijacked by it.

Let me show you another case.

Barack Obama's first debate against Mitt Romney in 2012. Obama was having a bad night—looking tired, disengaged, less sharp than his challenger. Romney was on. Crisp, confident, prepared. The contrast was obvious.

The narrative around that debate was intensely negative for Obama. It lasted for days. Weeks, really. A significant share of political commentary treated it as a potential turning point in a race that had, until that moment, leaned clearly in Obama's favor.

Obama won the election by nearly four percentage points three weeks later.

His national polling average dipped briefly after the debate—the dip is real—then recovered. The debate mattered. It likely narrowed Obama's margin somewhat. But the full record of the race—the underlying economy, Obama's incumbency advantage, Romney's struggles with key demographic groups, fundamentals that had been in place for months—mattered more.

The narrative in the week following that first debate didn't reflect that balance. It treated the debate as revelatory. Game-changing. The moment the race fundamentally shifted.

The narrative overweighted the recent event relative to the accumulated evidence. The electorate, when it actually voted, weighted things differently.

Here's what I want you to sit with, because this is where the real cost lives.

This dynamic doesn't just shape how outside observers judge candidates. It shapes how elected officials assess their own policies once implemented. It shapes what they choose to do, and when they choose to do it.

A policy enacted several years earlier, whose effects unfold gradually and are difficult to attribute cleanly, competes for attention against whatever happened most recently. A news story from this morning. A constituent complaint from yesterday. A poll number from last week.

The old policy sits in a structurally disadvantaged position—the same one we've seen in every other domain this book has examined.

An official assessing "how is this policy working" faces the same distortion a manager faces when evaluating an employee's year. The honest full-record answer requires assembling evidence spread unevenly across time, some of it no longer vivid, some of it difficult to measure. The recency-weighted answer is just whatever impression happens to be freshest at the moment the assessment gets made.

Which answer do you think wins most of the time?

Policy scholars who've written historical retrospectives on major legislative initiatives have noted a failure mode tied directly to electoral cycles. Policies whose genuine benefits take longer than one election cycle to materialize get systematically underweighted in real-time political evaluation, compared to policies offering immediate, visible results. This happens independent of which set of policies actually produces better long-run outcomes.

This is the walk-year contract mistake applied to governance. Voters reward whatever produced a vivid, recent, favorable result. They underweight investments whose payoff hasn't arrived yet, or arrived too long ago to remain vivid—regardless of which category of investment actually served the public interest better across a longer horizon.

Infrastructure offers the cleanest example.

A bridge built early in an official's term, now functioning quietly and effectively, competes for credit against a ribbon-cutting ceremony held two weeks before the election. The ceremony gets the press coverage. The ceremony gets remembered. The ceremony gets the photo on the campaign mailer that lands in your mailbox the weekend before you vote.

The bridge that's been working without incident for three years? It gets forgotten—even though the bridge might represent better long-term resource allocation than whatever project generated the late-term photo opportunity.

You know what happens when you see this pattern clearly? You start noticing it everywhere. You start seeing officials time announcements to land in the final stretch. Delay groundbreakings. Hold completed projects back from opening so the ribbon-cutting lands in the right month, the right week.

Not because they're corrupt. Not because they don't care about good governance. Because they understand, correctly, that voters weight recent events more heavily than the full record—and governing accordingly is how you stay in office long enough to do anything at all.

Ford lost by two points. The Poland gaffe aired six weeks before the election. Nothing he said in those six weeks moved the needle.

Chapter 7: How the Story Ends

In 1993, a patient at Toronto General Hospital lay on their side while a gastroenterologist threaded a colonoscope through their colon. The procedure took eight minutes. The patient turned a dial every sixty seconds to register how much it hurt right then. Peak pain: seven out of ten. Final minute: still seven.

The colonoscopy patients weren't rating the procedure—they were rating the memory of the final minute, the same way the Angels weren't signing Pujols, they were signing their memory of 2011.

Another patient, same week, same hospital, same procedure. This one took twenty-four minutes—triple the duration. Same dial, same sixty-second intervals. Peak pain: also seven. But the final minute registered a two.

Three weeks later, both patients answered one question: Overall, how bad was it?

The eight-minute patient rated their experience worse. Significantly worse. Even though they'd endured less total pain—one-third the time, same peak intensity, objectively less cumulative suffering—it didn't matter. The longer procedure ended gently. That's what stuck.

Donald Redelmeier and Daniel Kahneman published this in 1996, and it should have broken something in how we think about evaluation. Memory doesn't add things up. It samples. Two moments, specifically: the worst part, and however it ended. Everything in between dissolves into background static you can't reliably retrieve.

They called it the peak-end rule, though Kahneman might as well have called it the December 31st rule, because we do this to everything—our jobs, our relationships, our own lives. We don't judge the whole experience. We judge the arbitrary endpoint, the boundary we happened to measure at, the moment someone asked us how it was going.

Redelmeier tested it directly in a follow-up. He had doctors leave the colonoscope in for an extra minute after the actual procedure finished, just sitting there doing nothing while the worst part was over and discomfort ebbed.

Patients rated it better. They were more likely to come back for their next screening.

Adding pain—literal, measurable, additional pain—improved the memory, because it changed what the ending felt like.

That's recency operating on your own experience of your own body lying on a table in a hospital gown.

I learned this the hard way watching my parents the summer I turned twenty-two. I was home from college for three months between graduating and starting a job. They'd been married twenty-six years by then. Twenty-six years I'd watched up close—the daily negotiation of two people sharing a life, mostly steady, occasionally tense, nothing extraordinary either way.

That summer my dad's business hit something. I still don't know exactly what—he didn't talk about it directly, and I was too young and too wrapped up in my own transition to ask the right questions. But the stress bled into everything. They fought more than I'd seen in years. Money, mostly. Tone of voice. Small things that weren't small.

I went back to school that fall convinced they were headed for divorce. Not because I had evidence. Because the last thing I'd seen was tension, and the last thing I'd seen rewrote everything that came before it.

They didn't divorce. The business thing resolved. They're still together. But for years afterward, if someone asked me what my parents' marriage was like, the first image that surfaced was that summer. Not the two decades of relative calm before it. The summer I watched them struggle became, in my memory, representative of the whole thing.

I was running the peak-end rule on my own parents without knowing it had a name.

This shows up everywhere, but the place it lands with the highest stakes is inside long relationships—the ones where you're deciding whether to stay.

Take two people who've been together four years. First three years: solid. They traveled well. They made each other laugh at weird moments. They got through hard stretches without weaponizing old arguments. Then year four got rough. Money tightened. Work stress spilled over. They started snapping at each other in ways they didn't used to. By month ten of year four, one of them was lying awake at 2 a.m. wondering if this was still working.

Ask that person whether the relationship has been good.

They won't average the four years. They'll remember year four. The answer comes from what's recent, what's loud, what hasn't decayed yet. And if the real question underneath is "should I stay," the decision gets made on a sample that wildly overrepresents the end and underrepresents the three years before it.

You might be thinking: well, year four *is* the present. Of course it should matter more—it's what's happening now, and what's happening now probably predicts what's coming next better than what happened three years ago.

But you're not asking whether year four predicts year five. You're asking whether the relationship is good. Your memory is answering a different question. It's not giving you the current trendline. It's giving you a summary of the whole thing, built almost entirely from the most recent chapter, whether or not that chapter is representative of anything beyond itself.

Flip it. Same couple, same rough year four, but in month eleven something shifts. The financial pressure eases. They take a weekend away and it's easy again—the kind of easy they'd forgotten they could be. They have one of those long late-night conversations that actually resolves something instead of just surfacing it. Month twelve feels better.

Ask them six months later how year four was.

They'll say it was hard, but they got through it. Maybe even that it made them stronger. The memory won't sum the pain of months one through ten against the relief of months eleven and twelve. The ending rewrites the story. A year that was mostly grinding and tense gets remembered as something they survived together, filed under "challenges we overcame," because the last chapter was reconnection and the last chapter is what memory samples when you ask it for a verdict.

Neither memory is lying. Both are systematically wrong.

This isn't the negativity bias, which would predict that bad information outweighs good information regardless of timing. A single brutal fight doesn't erase ten warm months because negative experiences are inherently stronger. It erases them because it happened last.

This also isn't loss aversion. The peak-end rule runs in both directions with equal force. A relationship that ends its bad year well gets overcredited just as reliably as a relationship that ends its good year badly gets undercredited. The bias doesn't care about valence—good or bad. It cares about position in the sequence.

That makes it particularly vicious in relationship decisions: whether to move in together, whether to marry, whether to leave, whether to try again after a breakup. These decisions almost always surface because something recent happened. You don't wake up on a random boring Tuesday in month seven and reconsider your entire relationship for no reason. You reconsider because you just had the worst fight in two years, or the best weekend in two years.

The decision arrives on the heels of whatever just happened, which means the evidence you're weighing is the evidence that's freshest—and least representative of the relationship as a whole.

Therapists who work with couples long-term know this. The good ones structure their intake to counteract it. They don't ask, "How have things been?" They ask, "Walk me through the last six months, week by week." They make you reconstruct the whole stretch, not summarize it from memory, because the summary will be wrong. It'll overweight the end.

A couple who shows up after three great weeks following nine hard months will say things have been getting better. A couple who shows up after three hard weeks following nine good months will say things have been falling apart. Both are answering from the same distorted sample, and both are about to make a major decision based on it.

The only real countermeasure is contemporaneous documentation—forcing yourself to record what's actually happening while it's happening, before memory has a chance to rewrite it. Some couples do this formally: a monthly check-in where they sit down and talk through what the last four weeks actually looked like, not what they remember it looking like. Others do it informally but consistently, revisiting the recent past with enough specificity that recent stuff can't dominate the whole picture.

You're forcing retrieval from the middle of the timeline, not just the end, before the middle has faded past the point where you can access it honestly.

Friendships break the same way, just quieter.

A friendship doesn't end with a lease expiring or a court filing. It fades. You stop texting as often. Plans get canceled, rescheduled, canceled again, and then neither of you suggests new ones. The friendship dies across a hundred small moments where one of you could have reached out and didn't.

And at each of those small moments, you're running the same calculation: Is this friendship still worth the effort it takes to maintain it?

The answer depends on what you remember the friendship feeling like. And what you remember depends on what it felt like last.

Say you haven't seen a close friend in four months—not because anything's wrong, just because life got busy and neither of you pushed hard enough to make it happen. Then you finally grab dinner, and it's warm. You laugh. You talk for three hours and leave thinking, "We're still close. This still works."

That warmth colors everything. The four months of drift don't register as a warning sign, because look how good it felt when you finally connected. You're overweighting the end. The friendship might actually be fading—four months is a long gap for people who live in the same city and claim to be close—but one good dinner makes you think it's fine.

Flip it. Same four months of normal, steady friendship—texts here and there, nothing intense but nothing wrong. Then you reach out to make plans and they take two days to respond. You meet up and it's fine, but not great. A little stilted. Conversation doesn't flow the way it used to. You leave thinking, "Maybe we're just in different places now."

You're still overweighting the end. The friendship didn't fundamentally change in those two days. But the sample you're drawing from has changed, and the sample is dominated by what's recent, and what's recent was lukewarm.

So you quietly underinvest in friendships that are still strong, because one recent interaction went flat. And you quietly overinvest in friendships that are already fading, because one recent interaction went well.

Neither decision gets made explicitly or consciously. You just drift toward or away, based on what the last interaction made you feel. And five years later you look up and realize you're still trying with someone where it hasn't actually worked in years, or you've lost touch with someone you genuinely valued because the drift started right after one weird dinner and you never course-corrected.

I have a friend—I'll call him Mark because that's his name—who I almost lost this way. We'd been close since college. Stood up in each other's weddings, knew each other's families, had years of history. Then we both moved, different cities, and for about eighteen months we barely talked. Not because anything was wrong. Just life. Work. Kids for him, career stuff for me. The friendship went quiet.

Then we happened to both be in the same city for work and grabbed a drink. And it was awkward. Not terrible—we didn't fight or anything—just off. We'd lost the thread of each other's lives. I didn't know what was happening with his job anymore. He didn't know what I was working on. We spent the first twenty minutes catching up on facts instead of actually connecting.

I left that drink thinking, "I guess we're not as close as we used to be."

That thought almost became self-fulfilling. I stopped reaching out as much. He probably did the same calculation from his end. We could have lost the friendship entirely, based on one mediocre drink that happened to be the most recent data point in an eighteen-month gap.

What saved it was dumb luck. His wife called my wife about something unrelated a few months later, and in that conversation it came up that we'd both been feeling weird about the friendship, both using that one drink as the referendum on whether it was still working. Once we named it out loud, we laughed—because of course one awkward drink after a year and a half of not seeing each other doesn't mean the friendship is dead. We made an actual effort after that. The friendship's fine now.

But it almost wasn't. And the only reason it survived is because we accidentally talked about it before the drift calcified into permanent distance.

Jobs do this too, and the stakes are your career—how you spend forty-plus hours a week, what you learn, who you become.

Say you've been at a company for four years. First three years were good. You grew. You liked your manager. You worked on projects that felt like they mattered, where you could see your work affecting real outcomes. Year four, the company reorganizes. Your manager leaves. You get assigned to a project you don't believe in—maybe you think it's solving the wrong problem, or solving the right problem badly—and you're now reporting to someone whose management style makes you tired. Every one-on-one feels like a performance review. Every decision takes three meetings.

Six months into year four, a recruiter calls.

You're going to assess whether to leave based on how the job has been. But "how the job has been" is going to be dominated by the last six months, not the first three years. The growth, the good manager, the meaningful projects—all of that is still in your work history, still shaped who you are professionally. But it's not in your memory with the same weight as the last six months of frustration.

The peak-end rule predicts you'll remember the job more negatively than an honest average would support, because the end is bad and the end is what you sample when someone asks you to summarize the experience.

That might still be the right call—maybe the reorganization is permanent, maybe this is what the job is now, and the first three years were the anomaly. But you won't know if you're deciding based on a representative sample or a recency-distorted one unless you deliberately reconstruct the fuller timeline before you decide.

The reverse happens just as often, and it's worse because you don't even realize you're learning the wrong lesson.

You spend three years miserable. Underpaid, overworked, misaligned with what the company actually values. You watch people get promoted for things that don't matter. You pitch ideas that die in meetings. Your manager doesn't advocate for you. You go home tired in a way that sleep doesn't fix.

You should leave. You know you should leave. But inertia is real, and leaving is hard, and you keep telling yourself it'll get better.

Then, in month thirty-nine, they offer you a promotion. Suddenly your manager is singing your praises. You get pulled into higher-level conversations. The last two months feel validating in a way the previous three years never did. You leave on good terms—maybe you're moving cities, or going back to school, or taking a role that's genuinely better—and your exit interview is warm.

Five years later, someone asks you about that job.

You'll describe it as a good experience. You'll remember it warmly. You might even seek out roles that look similar, because your memory of what that job was like is dominated by how it ended, and how it ended was validation and respect and an ego boost.

The three years of being ground down are still in there somewhere. But they've faded. They're not what surfaces when you summarize the experience. And that means the lesson you extracted from your own life is backwards.

You spent three years in a place that didn't value you, that burned you out, that made you smaller instead of bigger. That experience should have taught you something about what to avoid—what it feels like when a workplace doesn't work for you, what red flags to watch for, how long is too long to wait for things to get better.

Instead, because the ending was good, your memory filed the whole thing under "positive experience." The lesson you walked away with was: stick it out, it'll turn around.

Maybe it will. But probably it won't. And now you're more likely to stay in the next bad situation longer than you should, because the last time you were in a bad situation it ended well, and endings are what memory uses to write the summary.

Think about what that costs you over a career. If you learn to tolerate bad jobs because one bad job happened to end well, you'll spend years in places that don't deserve you. You'll miss opportunities because you're still waiting for the turnaround. You'll undervalue yourself because you've internalized that the right move is to wait it out.

And it all traces back to one distorted sample—a memory that let the final chapter overwrite the previous thirty-six.

Vacations show the cleanest version of this because they're bounded and you usually evaluate them right after they end. A week-long trip can be fantastic for six days—beautiful weather, great food, easy companionship, the kind of days where you're not checking your phone because you don't need to be anywhere but where you are.

Then the last day goes wrong. Flight delayed six hours. Argument with your travel partner in the airport over something stupid that wouldn't have mattered if you weren't both exhausted. You get home drained and frustrated, and the vacation you were just on—the one that was great for six straight days—now feels tainted.

Two weeks later, someone asks how the trip was.

You'll say it was fine, maybe good, but the flight home was a nightmare. The six great days won't be lost entirely—you'll remember they happened—but they won't dominate the summary the way they would if the trip had ended on a great day. The ending overwrites the average.

Researchers have tested this directly with multi-day experiences. They have people rate each day of a vacation in real time, then rate the whole vacation retrospectively after it ends. The retrospective rating correlates more strongly with the last day's rating than with the average of all the days, even when the last day was an obvious outlier.

Your memory doesn't care that it's an outlier. It cares that it came last.

Some experience designers have figured this out and started building around it. Customer service teams that track satisfaction scores know that a support interaction's ending matters more than its middle. A call that starts with a long hold and a frustrating transfer but ends with a genuinely helpful agent who resolves your issue will get rated better than a call that starts smoothly but ends with the problem unresolved. The total time wasted might be identical. The ending determines the score.

Some companies use this well: they train agents to close every call warmly, make sure the last thing a customer hears is confirmation that the problem is handled, structure the final minute to feel like resolution even when the middle was rocky.

Other companies use it cynically. They know they can bury friction in the middle of a process—a confusing form, an annoying upsell, an extra step that shouldn't be there—and smooth it over with a polished final screen that says "You're all set!" in friendly sans-serif over a cheerful gradient. The user forgets the friction. The final screen is what sticks.

The peak-end rule becomes a tool for getting people to tolerate bad design, as long as the bad design doesn't happen at the end.

You see this in product onboarding, subscription cancellations, checkout flows. The companies that have absorbed the research make the last step feel easy and affirming, even when the steps before it were deliberately frustrating, because they know the end is what you'll remember when someone asks if the experience was good.

So here's the question the chapter has been building toward, the one you're probably already asking yourself: if the peak-end rule is this powerful, if it rewrites how we remember our own relationships and jobs and friendships and vacations, what is it doing to how we judge our investments?

You hold a stock for eighteen months. It trades sideways for most of that time—some up days, some down days, nothing dramatic. Then it rallies hard in the final month. When you look back at that position, you won't remember it as boring. You'll remember it as a winner, because it ended up.

Or you hold it for eighteen months, mostly flat, then it drops fifteen percent in the final three weeks. You'll remember that position as a mistake, even if it was fine for the first seventeen months.

The same pattern, the same total return, remembered completely differently depending on which direction it was moving when you happened to check.

And the thing is—you probably are going to check. You're going to evaluate the position, decide whether to hold or sell, build a story about whether your analysis was right. And the story you build will be dominated by the end, because that's what's recent, and recent is what feels real.

Twenty-four minutes of pain ending at a two felt better in memory than eight minutes ending at a seven. Not because the patients were confused or irrational. Because memory samples the peak and the end, and duration barely factors in.

You're about to do the same thing with every position you hold. The question isn't whether the peak-end rule will distort your judgment. The question is whether you'll notice it happening before you make the decision it's pushing you toward.

The shorter procedure with the worse ending got the worse rating. Both patients experienced the same peak pain. Only the ending differed.

Chapter 8: What Got Cited Last

Open Google Scholar right now and search for any topic you care about. Notice what loads first: the newest papers, sorted by publication date, as if recency were a proxy for relevance. You're about to cite the same way millions of researchers cite every day—and you're about to make the same mistake.

Powell's 'transitory' was a forecast based on the most recent inflation data, exactly the way Sarah Chen's literature review was built from the most recent publications. Both mistook the last data point for the trend.

The top twenty entries are all from the past three years. One paper from 2019 has been cited 847 times. Another from 2021 has 412 citations. Both address exactly the question her grant proposal is asking. She clicks the first one. Skims it. Adds it to her citation manager. Opens the second. Does the same. Scrolls down. Finds a 2020 paper, a 2022 paper, a 2023 paper. Her citation list grows. Seventeen sources now, all published in the last four years, all actively discussed at the conference she attended last month.

The review section is taking shape. She can see the finish line.

What she does not have—because she never scrolled past the first three pages of results, because her database defaulted to sorting by recency, because her field's recent work is what her advisor mentioned and what her colleagues are currently citing—is a 1987 paper that established the very framework every one of those recent papers is built on. Methodologically rigorous. Foundational. Ran a larger sample than most of the newer studies.

It will not appear in her literature review. Not because she evaluated it and found it wanting. Because she never saw it at all.

You might be thinking: but she's a professional researcher. Shouldn't she know to look deeper?

She does know. She also has fourteen days left, three other deadlines this month, and a database that surfaces what's newest first. This is how literature reviews get assembled. In every field. By researchers working under real time constraints with tools designed to privilege what arrived most recently. And it's happening in the one domain we built specifically to be immune to exactly this problem.

Science is supposed to be different.

The field's entire methodological identity rests on the claim that a finding's age is irrelevant to its truth value. A well-designed study from 1985 should carry the same evidential weight as an equally well-designed study from 2023, once both have been properly assessed. That's the standard. That's what separates scientific synthesis from a political campaign's opposition research file or a cable news segment's framing of yesterday's poll.

It's also—researchers who study how science actually gets produced have found—a standard the field's own practices do not consistently meet.

This chapter sits here, at this specific point in the book's sequence, because science's self-image as the one discipline immune to recency bias is what makes the finding worth dwelling on. A courtroom does not claim to be immune. We saw in Chapter 3 a legal system that structurally amplifies recency through rules governing witness order and closing arguments. A political campaign does not claim immunity either—the professionals running one openly plan around the last-impression effect we've traced through eight domains.

But science? Science explicitly commits, in its stated norms and peer-review standards, to weighing evidence independent of when it arrived.

Which makes it the perfect test case. If the recency-weighted pattern shows up here—in the field designed specifically to guard against it—then we're not looking at a symptom of any one domain's particular incentives or institutional sloppiness. We're looking at something closer to a default condition of how human attention works, one that even the most methodologically careful disciplines have to fight against deliberately.

The pattern shows up most clearly in how researchers construct literature reviews: the sections of papers, grant proposals, and textbooks that synthesize what a field currently understands about a given question. These reviews are supposed to weigh the full relevant body of research on methodological merits, regardless of publication date.

That's the ideal.

In practice? Researchers who study citation patterns across large bodies of academic literature have repeatedly observed a tilt toward citing recently published work more heavily than an evenhanded weighting of quality alone would predict. The finding is consistent across fields. Documented in medicine, psychology, economics, ecology. It has its own minor subfield within the study of how science operates as a social system.

The magnitude varies by field and by study design, and I'm not going to attach a specific percentage to it here, because the honest version of the claim is qualitative: recent publications attract citation attention disproportionate to what a purely quality-based weighting would predict. Older work—including, in documented cases, foundational or field-defining older work—receives less citation traffic than its rigor or importance would justify on the merits alone.

Walk through how this actually happens. Not in some imaginary worst-case scenario, but in the ordinary mechanics of assembling a literature review under real conditions.

A researcher begins by searching current databases. PubMed if you're in medicine. PsycINFO in psychology. Google Scholar across disciplines. The tools of contemporary scholarship are structured to surface what is newest first, in the same way a search engine or social media feed defaults to recency as an organizing principle.

Which means the researcher's very first pass through the relevant literature is already weighted—by the tools' own design, before any deliberate judgment about quality has even been applied—toward what was published most recently.

An older, foundational paper sits further down in a search result ordered by recency. Requires more deliberate effort to locate and retrieve. And competes, once found, against a stack of more recent papers that are—by simple virtue of their currency—more likely to be actively discussed among the researcher's own peer network, cited in whatever conference she attended last month, and therefore easier to recall without the friction of digging back through older, less immediately available work.

Here's the mechanism problem, the part that makes this more than just individual researcher carelessness.

A review committee drafting a literature review section for a grant proposal. Four researchers. Working under a real and ordinary time constraint—the proposal is due in three weeks, they're all teaching, two of them have data-collection obligations for other projects. They assemble their citation list substantially from the most recent two or three years of published work in their subfield.

Not out of any deliberate decision to exclude older material. But because the recent material is what surfaces first in a database search ordered by date. What colleagues are discussing in the current moment. What fits most easily into the tight timeline they're drafting under.

An older study—methodologically rigorous, sample size comparable to or exceeding more recent work—remains unmentioned. Not judged inferior. Just never encountered during the recency-weighted search process that generated the final citation list.

Now here's what that pattern costs, compounded across an entire field's understanding over time. And I mean *costs*—not in some abstract sense, but in wasted effort, in questions that never get asked, in researchers spending years re-establishing what their field already knew.

Think about what happens when you miss the foundation someone else already laid. You don't just lose time. You lose the chance to build on top of it—to ask the next question instead of re-answering the first one.

A field that consistently underweights older work in its ongoing synthesis of "what we currently know" risks a specific and somewhat ironic failure mode: rediscovering findings that an earlier generation of researchers had already established. Sometimes rigorously. Simply because the newer generation's literature reviews never surfaced the older work clearly enough for it to inform the newer research design.

I first encountered this pattern while working on something completely unrelated—a meta-analysis of intervention studies in educational psychology. We were following proper systematic review protocol, which meant searching back twenty years instead of just looking at recent work. And we kept finding these pairs: a 2019 study reporting some finding as novel, and a 1998 study that had found essentially the same thing, often with a larger sample.

Not once. Repeatedly.

The 2019 studies weren't fraudulent. The researchers weren't sloppy. They'd done literature reviews, cited recent work, had their papers peer-reviewed by experts in the field. The older studies simply weren't in anyone's active awareness anymore. They'd fallen out of the citation stream. And so an entire generation of researchers spent time, grant money, and effort rediscovering things the field had already figured out two decades earlier.

Picture what that actually looks like on the ground. A graduate student—let's call her Maria, because I watched this exact sequence play out with someone I know—spends two years designing a study on how feedback timing affects learning outcomes in online education. She runs a careful literature review. Finds recent papers on feedback, on online learning, on timing effects. Designs her study to address what looks like a genuine gap: nobody in the recent literature has tested whether immediate versus delayed feedback matters differently in asynchronous online courses than it does in real-time classroom settings.

She gets funding. Recruits participants. Runs the study. Finds that immediate feedback produces better learning outcomes in the online setting, but the effect is smaller than what earlier classroom studies had found. She writes it up. Publishes it. The paper gets cited. It's a genuine contribution to the field's current understanding.

Three years later, someone doing deep historical work on feedback research finds a 1994 dissertation—never widely published, sitting in a university library archive—that tested exactly this question. Same design. Larger sample. Same finding: immediate feedback works in online settings, but the effect size is smaller than in face-to-face instruction. The dissertation explained why: in asynchronous environments, students can control the pacing, which partially compensates for delayed feedback in ways that don't happen in real-time classroom settings.

Maria's study wasn't wrong. It was redundant. She spent two years and a chunk of grant money re-establishing something the field had already figured out, because the earlier work had fallen out of the citation stream and never surfaced in her literature review. The database didn't show it. Her advisor didn't mention it. The peer reviewers who evaluated her paper before publication didn't catch it.

Not because anyone was careless. Because the older work had aged out of the recency-weighted awareness that shapes what gets searched, what gets cited, what gets remembered as "the current state of knowledge."

And here's what that cost Maria specifically, beyond the wasted time: she could have built on that 1994 finding. Could have asked the *next* question—tested whether certain types of pacing control matter more than others, or whether the effect varies by subject matter, or whether you can design delayed feedback that preserves the benefits while accommodating asynchronous schedules. Instead, she spent her dissertation re-answering the first question, and the field lost whatever the second question might have revealed.

Historians of science who examine specific cases of this rediscovery pattern describe it as a recurring cost of recency-weighted scholarship. But "cost" feels abstract until you see it from the researcher's side. You've just spent two years of your life, you've produced something genuinely rigorous, and then you find out someone else already did it. That's not just inefficiency. That's your early career—your shot at making a name, at contributing something new—spent duplicating work that would have been available to you if the search tools and citation practices had surfaced it.

The field spent resources, time, and researcher effort re-establishing something it already knew. That's the cost you can measure.

But there's a second cost, harder to quantify but more consequential: the questions that never get studied at all because they fell out of recent discussion.

Sketch a graduate student choosing a dissertation topic. A genuinely rigorous, field-agnostic approach to that choice would weigh the full landscape of open questions in a discipline on their merits. Which gaps in existing knowledge are important, tractable, and underexplored, independent of how recently the surrounding literature happened to be published.

In practice?

A student's sense of what counts as an exciting, fundable, publishable question is shaped substantially by whatever a small number of recent, widely discussed papers in the field have made visible. Those are the papers assigned in recent seminars. Cited in recent job talks. Referenced by the grant announcements the student's advisor is most likely to mention.

A genuinely important older question that fell out of active discussion for reasons having nothing to do with its importance—a change in available methods, a senior researcher's retirement, a funding priority that shifted for unrelated administrative reasons—is considerably less likely to reach a new student's attention at all.

Not because anyone evaluated it and found it wanting. Because it never surfaced in the recency-ordered stream of material that shaped the student's sense of the field's live questions in the first place.

We don't study what's important. We study what's recent enough to register as important within the narrow window of discussion our search tools and conference schedules make visible. And we do this while genuinely believing we're choosing topics on their intellectual merits, because the distortion happens upstream of any conscious evaluation—in which questions reach our awareness at all.

I saw this play out in a field I followed closely for years. In the early 2000s, there was genuinely interesting work being done on how people learn from worked examples versus problem-solving practice. Rigorous studies. Clear findings. Then funding shifted toward digital learning tools, the senior researchers who'd been driving the worked-example research retired or moved to other topics, and by 2015 you could attend a major education research conference and not hear the question mentioned once.

The question didn't get answered. It just fell out of fashion.

A student starting a dissertation in 2018 would have no idea that entire body of work existed unless they happened to have an advisor who remembered it, or unless they did the kind of deep historical literature search that nobody has time for when they're also teaching and trying to finish in a fundable timeline. So the question just... sat there. Unresolved. Important. Invisible.

And here's the thing that makes this particularly hard to fix: the student doesn't experience this as a loss. They're excited about the questions that *did* surface in their recent seminar readings. Those questions feel live, current, important—because they're the ones people are talking about. The student isn't making a bad choice. They're making the only choice available to them, given the recency-filtered view of the field that their tools and their training environment have surfaced.

But the field loses the cumulative depth it could have built if each generation of researchers could actually see the full landscape of open questions instead of just the slice that happened to be recently discussed.

Now think about what you personally miss when you operate this way. Not as a researcher—most of us aren't—but in whatever domain you're making decisions in.

You're hiring. The candidate's most recent role is at a well-known company, doing work that maps cleanly to what you need. Their resume goes to the top of the pile.

What you don't see, because you stopped reading at the recent stuff that felt relevant, is that seven years ago they built the exact system you're trying to build now, at a smaller company you've never heard of, and they did it better than anyone's done it since. That experience isn't missing from their resume. It's sitting right there in the middle section you skimmed past because it wasn't recent and the recent stuff already felt like enough.

You just hired someone who can do the job competently based on their recent work, and you missed the candidate who could have done it brilliantly based on their older, less visible experience. The information was right in front of you. Your attention just never landed on it, because the recent material looked sufficient and you had thirty other resumes to review before the end of the day.

Or you're researching a business decision. The newest analysis on the topic is eighteen months old, written by a consulting firm everyone in your industry follows. Clear. Well-presented. Answers the exact question you're asking. You base your strategy on it.

What you don't realize is that a smaller firm published a more thorough analysis four years ago, covering edge cases and failure modes the recent report didn't address, based on a longer historical dataset. It's not in your awareness because it doesn't show up in a Google search sorted by date, and none of your peers mentioned it at the last conference. The information was available. You just never encountered it, because your search process was weighted—by tool design, by peer discussion, by your own constrained attention—toward what arrived most recently.

This is what recency bias actually costs you. Not wrong decisions, necessarily. But decisions made from an artificially narrowed information base that you experienced as complete, because the narrowing happened before you ever started evaluating the material.

You thought you were weighing all the relevant evidence. You were weighing all the evidence that made it through a recency filter you didn't know was running.

Let me be specific about what this looked like in my own work, because I've done this—made a decision based on what felt like a complete picture that turned out to be just the recent picture.

A few years ago I was advising a team building out a new product feature. We did our research. Looked at what competitors were doing. Read the recent case studies. The consensus from everything published in the last two years was clear: users wanted this particular interaction pattern. Every recent article, every conference talk, every product teardown pointed the same direction.

We built it that way.

Six months later, usage was underwhelming. Not terrible, but not what we'd projected. I was digging through some older material for an unrelated project when I found a 2014 research report—published by a firm that no longer existed, not indexed in the places I'd searched—that had tested this exact interaction pattern extensively. Their finding: users said they wanted it in surveys, but didn't actually use it in practice. The report recommended a different approach, one we'd considered and dismissed because none of the recent literature supported it.

The information was out there. We'd just never seen it, because our research process was weighted toward recent publications and our tools surfaced recent material first. We spent six months building something that matched the current consensus while missing the older, more rigorous evidence that the current consensus was wrong.

That's the shape of the cost. Not catastrophic failure. Just wasted time and effort and money solving a problem someone else had already solved, in a way we would have chosen if we'd known their work existed.

And here's the part that makes this particularly insidious: it doesn't feel like you're missing anything.

The recent material is coherent. Discusses the current state of the question. Cites other recent work. Forms a complete-seeming picture. There's no obvious gap. No moment where you think, "I should probably look back further." The recent literature forms a self-contained, internally consistent bubble of discussion that gives no signal it's incomplete.

You're not ignoring contrary evidence. You're making a decision based on what looks like all the available evidence, and the only reason it looks that way is because the search process filtered out the older material before you ever got a chance to evaluate it.

This is different from the patterns we saw in earlier chapters, where the recency weighting was at least somewhat transparent. A stock trader watching the latest price tick knows they're watching recent data. A political commentator reacting to the newest poll understands they're responding to fresh information. The recency is visible.

Here? The recency is hidden inside the search process itself. You experience the output—the list of papers, the stack of resumes, the set of case studies—as "the relevant material," not as "the relevant material that happened to pass through a recency filter." The filter is invisible. Which makes it much harder to correct for.

Because when you can see the filter, you can at least try to compensate. You can remind yourself that the latest poll isn't necessarily predictive, that the most recent performance review might not represent the employee's full capability. You're aware that you're looking at a slice, and you can consciously work to expand your view.

But when the filter is built into the tools you're using to gather information—when the database automatically sorts by date, when the search algorithm privileges recent content, when your professional network's discussions naturally center on whatever just came out—you don't even know you're looking at a slice. You think you're looking at the whole picture. And that makes you confident in decisions that are actually based on incomplete information.

There's a professional-incentive layer to this that parallels the dynamics we've already seen in economic forecasting and political commentary, and it's worth stating plainly because it makes the pattern self-reinforcing.

Academic publishing and citation metrics reward novelty in ways built directly into how researchers' careers are evaluated. Citation counts—a widely used and heavily weighted measure of a paper's influence and a researcher's professional standing—accrue disproportionately to recent, actively discussed work.

Which means researchers have a direct professional incentive to engage with and cite the current literature their peer community is discussing, independent of any conscious decision to privilege recency over quality.

A researcher who builds a career's citation record around engaging deeply with older, historically important but less currently fashionable work may produce genuinely more rigorous scholarship while accumulating fewer of the citation metrics that shape hiring, promotion, and grant decisions inside the modern academic institution.

It's the same asymmetric-cost pattern we identified in the sports front office that pays socially for correctly discounting a hot streak, and in the forecaster who bears career risk for correctly resisting an extrapolative consensus.

The professional cost of being right in an unfashionable direction exceeds the professional benefit.

Which means the individually rational choice—for a researcher trying to build a sustainable career—is to tilt toward engaging with whatever the field is currently discussing, even when a more patient historical engagement would produce better science.

I watched a colleague navigate this exact tradeoff a few years back. Brilliant researcher. Tenure-track. Doing genuinely original work that required engaging deeply with an older body of literature most of the field had moved past. The work was rigorous. Important. But it wasn't accumulating citations at the rate the tenure committee expected, because the questions she was asking weren't the questions the field was currently excited about.

Her annual review was clear about the problem. Not in so many words—they didn't say "your work isn't trendy enough." But the feedback was consistent: strong methodological work, but limited impact as measured by citation metrics and conference visibility. She needed to demonstrate broader influence in the field.

She adjusted. Started working on problems closer to the current conversation. Her citation rate went up. She got tenure.

I'm not criticizing her choice—she made the rational career move given the incentives she was facing. But the field lost something when those incentives pushed her away from the harder, less fashionable work she'd been doing. And she's not unique. This is the systematic pressure every early-career researcher faces: align with the current discussion or risk professional survival.

The incentive structure doesn't just reward recent work. It punishes deep engagement with older work by making it professionally costlier to pursue.

And once you see that pattern, you start seeing it everywhere. Not just in academic research, but in any domain where professional advancement is tied to visible engagement with current discussion.

A consultant who builds a practice around applying lessons from older, less-discussed case studies is harder to market than one who can speak fluently about whatever framework went viral on LinkedIn last month. A manager who hires based on a candidate's full career arc instead of their most recent role has to do more work to justify the decision to leadership. An investor who bases strategy on longer historical patterns instead of recent market commentary has to spend more time explaining why they're not following the current consensus.

In each case, the professionally safer move—the one that requires less justification, that aligns with what peers are currently discussing—is to weight recent information more heavily. Not because anyone believes recent information is more predictive. Because it's more *legible* as a basis for decision-making within the current professional environment.

We're not choosing recent information because we think it's better. We're choosing it because choosing it is easier to defend, easier to explain, more aligned with what everyone else is currently paying attention to. And then we convince ourselves, after the fact, that the recent information must have been the most relevant—because if it weren't, why would everyone be focusing on it?

The recency bias doesn't just come from tools or time constraints. It comes from the social and professional structures that make recent information the path of least resistance.

Now, you might be thinking: isn't peer review supposed to catch this?

It is. That's the mechanism. A paper goes out to expert reviewers before publication; those reviewers flag gaps, omissions, methodological problems. If a literature review is tilted too heavily toward recent work and missing foundational older studies that ought to be cited, a good reviewer should catch that and send the paper back for revision.

In theory.

In practice, peer reviewers are themselves researchers embedded in the same recency-weighted search and citation environment as the authors they're reviewing. A reviewer who is not personally familiar with an older, foundational study—because that study fell out of active discussion before the reviewer entered the field, or because the reviewer's own training emphasized recent work—is not going to flag its absence from a literature review they're evaluating.

The reviewer can only catch omissions they recognize as omissions. Which requires them to be aware of the older work in the first place. And if the field's citation practices have already allowed that work to fall out of common awareness, most reviewers won't be.

I've been on both sides of this. As an author, I've had papers accepted with literature reviews that I later realized were missing important older work—work I didn't know about at the time, and that none of my reviewers flagged. As a reviewer, I've read papers and thought "this literature review looks thorough" only to discover later, through unrelated reading, that there was a whole body of older research relevant to the paper's question that neither I nor the authors had been aware of.

Peer review works when the reviewers know what should be there. It doesn't work when the thing that should be there has already fallen out of collective awareness.

So the filter that keeps older work from being cited isn't just operating at the author level. It's operating at the reviewer level too. And at the editor level—the person deciding which reviewers to send the paper to in the first place. Everyone in the chain is working from the same recency-weighted view of what constitutes "the relevant literature" in their field.

Which means the quality-control mechanism that's supposed to catch these gaps is itself subject to the same bias it's supposed to be catching.

This is the part where I should probably offer you a clean framework for fixing it. A three-step process for expanding your information base, a checklist for catching recency filters before they narrow your decisions. That's what this chapter is supposed to deliver.

But I don't have a clean framework. What I have is a recognition that this is harder to fix than the other patterns we've looked at, precisely because the filter is invisible and the professional incentives work against correcting it.

What I can offer—and this is less satisfying than a framework, but it's what actually works—is a set of specific friction points you can build into your own search and decision processes. Small deliberate obstacles that force you to look past the recent material before you conclude you've seen enough.

Start here: before you finalize any decision based on recent information, set a mandatory pause. Not a long one—even five minutes works. And in that pause, ask yourself one question: "What would I need to know from before this recent material to change my conclusion?"

Not "is there anything older I should look at?" That's too open-ended. You'll answer "probably not" and move on.

Ask specifically: what *kind* of older information, if it existed, would make you decide differently?

For a literature review: what foundational methodology paper, if it existed, would change how you're framing the question?

For a hiring decision: what older role on this resume, if it were directly relevant, would make this candidate more qualified than the recent work suggests?

For a business strategy: what older case study or analysis, if it covered the failure modes you're worried about, would make you choose a different approach?

Frame it as a hypothetical. And then—this is the part that actually creates friction—spend ten minutes actively searching for that specific thing. Not a comprehensive historical review. Just ten minutes looking for the particular type of older information that would matter if it existed.

You won't always find it. But the act of looking trains you to notice when your information base is artificially narrowed by recency. And often enough, you will find something—not always the exact thing you hypothesized, but something older and relevant that your initial search missed.

A senior researcher I know does this with a physical timer. Before she finalizes a literature review, she sets a timer for fifteen minutes and forces herself to search explicitly for work published more than ten years ago that might be relevant. She doesn't always find anything. But the practice keeps her from falling into the "recent work feels complete" trap.

A hiring manager I worked with built a similar rule into his process: before making an offer, he makes himself identify one piece of older experience on the candidate's resume that he initially skimmed past, and he asks about it in a final conversation. Not as a gotcha. As a genuine check on whether he missed something by focusing too heavily on the recent roles.

These aren't frameworks. They're friction. Small, deliberate obstacles to the recency-weighted default. And they work not by guaranteeing you'll find the older information—sometimes there isn't any—but by making you aware that you might be looking at an incomplete picture even when the recent material feels sufficient.

The other piece—and this one is harder because it runs against professional incentives—is to build some small, visible space in your work for engaging with older material even when it's not currently fashionable.

If you're a researcher: cite one foundational older paper in every literature review, even if it's not what your field is currently discussing. Make it visible that you looked back.

If you're making hiring decisions: write one interview question that explicitly asks about older experience, something from earlier in the candidate's career that might not be top-of-mind in a conversation focused on recent work.

If you're doing market research: add one older case study or analysis to every brief you prepare, something from before the recent consensus formed, even if you ultimately follow the recent consensus.

This won't fix the systemic incentive problems. You're still operating in an environment that rewards recent engagement and makes older work professionally costlier to pursue. But it creates a small, visible counter-pressure. And if enough people do it, it starts to shift what counts as "thorough" in your field—from "covered the recent discussion" to "covered the recent discussion and checked whether older work still matters."

The goal isn't to privilege older information over recent information. The goal is to stop letting the tools and incentives make that choice for you before you even get a chance to evaluate it.

Because here's what we're actually doing when we let recency filters run invisibly: we're outsourcing our judgment about what information matters to whoever designed the search algorithm, to whatever professional incentives happen to be shaping current discussion, to the arbitrary fact of what got published or discussed most recently.

And then we're experiencing the output of that filter as our own considered evaluation of the full landscape of relevant information.

We're not weighing the evidence and concluding that recent work matters most. We're seeing only the recent work, concluding it's sufficient because it feels complete, and never realizing that the completeness is an artifact of the filter, not a property of the information itself.

That's the thing to notice. Not in some abstract sense, but in the next actual decision you make where you're basing your conclusion on what looks like a thorough review of available information.

Ask yourself: did you see the whole landscape, or just the part that surfaced recently enough to make it through the tools and incentives that shaped what reached your attention?

And if the answer is “I don’t know”—which is the honest answer more often than we’d like to admit—then you know where the gap is. Not in your evaluation. In what you saw before you started evaluating.

The filter runs first. Your judgment runs second. And everything that follows is only as complete as what the filter let through.

The practical question, then, isn’t whether you can eliminate the filter. You can’t. The volume of information in any domain worth thinking about exceeds what any single person could process in a lifetime. Filters are structural necessities, not optional conveniences.

The question is whether you can become aware of *which* filter is running, and what it systematically excludes.

This is harder than it sounds, because the filter doesn’t announce itself. When you pull up search results, read a curated newsletter, scroll a feed, or review citations in a paper, you’re not presented with a disclaimer that says: “The following represents approximately 0.02% of relevant material, selected according to criteria that prioritize recency, virality, institutional affiliation, and whatever happened to get linked from sources our algorithm already trusts.”

You just see the results. And because they look like a complete set—because they fill the screen, answer the question, provide enough material to form a judgment—your mind treats them as if they *are* the complete set.

This is where the distortion happens. Not in dishonesty, but in invisibility.

The older paper that's more rigorous but less cited doesn't appear on your radar not because it's less true, but because it's less recent. The dissenting expert who wrote the definitive critique in 2008 doesn't make it into your consideration set not because their argument is weaker, but because the debate moved on and the algorithm moved with it. The comprehensive dataset that contradicts the viral headline sits in an institutional repository that your search never queries, not because it's less reliable, but because it's formatted differently and hosted somewhere the index doesn't prioritize.

None of this is secret. The mechanisms are known. But knowing the mechanism doesn't change what you see when you actually sit down to research a question. You still see what the filter surfaces. And if you're like most people, you work with what you see.

The alternative—attempting to identify and audit every filtering mechanism between you and the information you'd need to form a complete picture—is functionally impossible for everyday decisions. You'd spend more time mapping the filter than evaluating the substance.

So the trap isn't that you're being misled. The trap is that you're being *partially* informed in a way that feels complete.

And the worst part is that the gap compounds.

Because the filter doesn't just affect what *you* see. It affects what everyone else saw when they wrote the papers you're reading, designed the studies you're citing, built the tools you're using. Their conclusions were shaped by the same recency-weighted, visibility-biased information environment. Which means when you rely on recent work to guide your thinking, you're not just accepting one filter—you're accepting a *cascade* of filters, each one narrowing the view a little more.

The systematic review you're reading was built on studies that were themselves built on literature reviews that prioritized what was accessible at the time. The policy recommendation you're evaluating was informed by think-tank reports that drew on datasets chosen for availability, not comprehensiveness. The expert opinion you're deferring to was formed in an information environment where the same recency bias that shapes your search results also shaped theirs.

This is how entire fields can drift toward a consensus that later turns out to have been built on an incomplete picture. Not because anyone was sloppy or dishonest, but because everyone was working with the same filtered view, and no one had the vantage point to see what was missing.

The correction, when it comes, usually doesn't come from someone doing better research within the existing filter. It comes from someone stepping outside it—pulling an old thread that had been dropped, running a query in a database no one was checking anymore, asking a question that had gone out of fashion.

And when that happens, the response is rarely: "Ah yes, we knew that gap existed; we just hadn't prioritized closing it." The response is usually surprise. Because the gap wasn't visible. The filter had smoothed it over so completely that its absence didn't register as absence—it just registered as the normal background state of knowledge.

Which brings us back to the practical problem.

If you can't eliminate the filter, and you can't feasibly audit it every time you need to make a judgment, what do you actually do?

The first move is simpler than it sounds: **assume incompleteness as the default.**

Not in a paralyzing, "I can never know anything" sense. In a calibrated sense. When you've done what feels like thorough research and arrived at a confident conclusion, add one additional step: ask yourself what would have to be true for this conclusion to be wrong, and whether that contradicting information would have made it through the filter you just used.

If the answer is no—if the information that would undermine your conclusion is old, obscure, formatted differently, hosted somewhere you didn't search, or published by people outside the networks your sources draw from—then you haven't done thorough research. You've done *filtered* research. Which might still be the best you can do given time and resource constraints, but it's not the same thing.

And recognizing that difference changes how you hold the conclusion.

The second move is to **diversify your filters.**

If you know that recency-weighted search is going to bias you toward the last five years of visible work, then deliberately add a pass that queries older material. If you know that algorithmic curation prioritizes virality, then deliberately seek out sources that optimize for something else—comprehensive archives, institutional repositories, domain-specific databases that don't care about engagement metrics.

This doesn't eliminate bias. It just ensures that you're not systematically exposed to only *one* kind of bias.

The third move, and maybe the most important one: **track your information sources the way you'd track your financial exposures.**

When you're building a conclusion—especially one that matters, one you're going to act on or advocate for—make a list of where the information came from. Not vague attributions like “research shows” or “experts say.” Specific sources. Which databases. Which journals. Which networks. Which time periods.

Then ask: if all of these sources shared a common filtering mechanism, what would that mechanism be? And what would it exclude?

If the answer is that they all prioritize the same thing—recency, prestige, virality, institutional access—then you’re not actually diversified. You’re just sampling from different parts of the same filtered set.

The goal isn’t to become paranoid or dismissive of what you find. The goal is to develop a reflex that asks: “What didn’t make it to me?” alongside “What did?”

Because the filter runs first. Always. And if you’re only interrogating what came through it, you’re starting your evaluation halfway through the process.

The question isn’t whether you saw enough to form *a* judgment. The question is whether you saw enough to trust that the judgment reflects the whole picture, and not just the part that happened to surface recently enough to stay visible.

The 1987 paper had been cited twice in the past five years. The 2021 paper with 412 citations said roughly the same thing. Sarah cited the recent one.

Chapter 9: Building the Longer Window

In December 2014, I sat across from Michael Chen in a conference room on the forty-second floor of a building in downtown Boston. Michael had built his manufacturing business over thirty years. He didn't like taking risks with the retirement money he'd finally started accumulating.

When I showed Michael Chen the energy thesis in December 2014, I was making the same mistake Bill Miller's investors made in 2005: I was counting from the wrong calendar, taking the most recent year's trend as the predictor.

I laid out the energy thesis. Global demand climbing. Production discipline holding across the major producers. OPEC maintaining quotas. The structural shift everyone had been waiting for finally arriving. And the proof, the part that made it feel not like speculation but like reading the obvious: eighteen straight months of double-digit returns across the energy sector. I had charts. I had momentum. I had a story that made recent performance feel like the beginning of something durable instead of what it actually was.

Michael said yes. We moved his portfolio overweight into energy stocks that week.

Oil crashed two months later. West Texas Intermediate went from $107 a barrel in June to $59 by December to $26 by February. The energy position lost a third of its value before I could even get him on the phone to discuss cutting it. By the time we did cut it, the damage was done.

He didn't yell. That would have been easier. He just said he was moving the account. He'd talked to a friend who'd recommended someone else. He appreciated what I'd done for him the first three years, but he needed to make a change.

I didn't lose Michael Chen because I made a forecast that turned out wrong. Everyone who works in markets long enough makes wrong forecasts, and clients who've survived a few cycles know that. I lost him because of how I'd built the forecast. I'd treated eighteen months of rising prices as evidence of a durable regime shift rather than what it actually was: a short, unrepresentative stretch of data sitting inside a much longer, much messier commodity cycle I could have examined if I'd bothered to pull it. The recent performance wasn't predictive. It was just recent. But recent felt real in a way the thirty-year history of oil price cycles—completely accessible, sitting in the same database I'd pulled the eighteen-month chart from—somehow didn't.

The energy thesis I'd walked in with wasn't even original. I'd absorbed it from the consensus that had formed across the analyst community in late 2014, and that consensus had formed the same way my own conviction had: everyone was staring at the same vivid eighteen-month run, and nobody was pulling back far enough to see what the longer pattern actually looked like. Supply was loosening. Demand signals were already shifting. The data was there. I just didn't weight it against the recent performance that felt so compelling.

That's the pattern this book has been circling for eight chapters, and it doesn't just show up in blown commodity calls.

A pension fund allocator chooses between two equity managers. One has delivered 12% annually over ten years. The other delivered 9% over the same decade but posted 18% last year. The allocator picks the second manager. They don't articulate it as recency bias. They articulate it as momentum, or skill finally showing through, or the manager hitting their stride. What they're actually doing is letting one recent year outweigh nine earlier ones, because the recent year is vivid and the nine-year average is abstract.

A software company's engineering manager sits down in December to write annual reviews. One engineer, Sarah, delivered consistently strong work from January through October—shipped three major features on time, mentored two junior developers, caught a critical bug in production that would have cost the company real money. But November and December were rough. She seemed distracted. Missed a deadline. The code review she submitted last week had sloppier work than usual. The manager doesn't pull her contributions from the full year. They reconstruct the year from memory, and what memory surfaces most easily is the last six weeks. The performance rating goes in a half-step lower than the full-year record would justify. Sarah doesn't get the promotion she expected. She starts looking. Four months later she accepts an offer from a competitor, and the manager is surprised, because he thought she'd seemed fine.

A jury in a civil trial hears four days of testimony. The plaintiff's key witness—a structural engineer who'd inspected the building and documented code violations—testified Tuesday morning. His testimony was detailed, technical, thirty pages of exhibits entered into evidence. The defense's final witness testified late Thursday afternoon. She was the contractor who'd done the work, and she was emotional, direct, and memorable. She cried on the stand. The jury deliberated Friday morning. Most of them didn't take notes during the trial. The judge didn't allow transcripts in the deliberation room. What they're weighing isn't the full trial. It's what they can retrieve unaided from memory, which means it's tilted—heavily, invisibly—toward the testimony that's still vivid. The engineer's thirty pages of documentation carry less weight in the room than the contractor's tears, not because the jurors are careless but because memory doesn't store everything equally.

A baseball front office evaluates two outfielders in free agency. Player A has averaged .280 with 22 home runs over eight seasons, including last year. Player B has averaged .270 with 19 home runs over the same span, but last year he hit .311 with 34 home runs—a clear career year, surrounded on both sides by performance closer to his actual baseline. The front office pays Player B $18 million a year. They pay Player A $12 million. Three years later, Player B has regressed to his career average and the contract is underwater. The front office didn't do bad math. They did recent math, and recent math feels more predictive than it is.

Different settings. Different stakes. Different timelines. Same mechanism every time.

First, a full, legitimately mixed history exists—ten years of fund performance, twelve months of employee contributions, four days of trial testimony, eight seasons of baseball statistics. Second, the most recent portion of that history becomes disproportionately easy to retrieve and disproportionately vivid at the exact moment a judgment has to be formed. And third, the judgment that gets made—without anyone involved consciously choosing to distort anything—ends up built from a badly unrepresentative sample of the record that was actually available.

You might think this is solvable. Just pay closer attention. Be more disciplined. Try harder.

I thought that too, for longer than I should have. But this book hasn't treated recency bias as a simple failure of effort or intelligence for a reason: it's rooted in how memory actually works. Human memory genuinely does retain recent, unrehearsed information more readily than older information of comparable importance. It's not a flaw. It's a feature. And it genuinely does respond—sensibly, on average—to the possibility that a recent change might signal a real regime shift rather than noise. A mind that gave equal weight to every piece of information it had ever encountered, regardless of when it was acquired, would be slower to detect real changes in the environment than the mind evolution actually built. It would miss turning points.

So the goal here isn't eliminating recency's influence on judgment. That's not possible, and it wouldn't be desirable if it were. The goal is correcting its proportion—making sure recent evidence counts for what it actually demonstrates, weighed fairly against the fuller record it sits inside, rather than counting as the whole record by default because it happens to be what surfaces first when you need to make a decision.

Here's what it costs when you don't correct it.

Not the abstract cost. The actual one.

Michael Chen didn't just move his account. He told people. That's how reputational damage works in wealth management—quietly at first, then all at once. I didn't get invited to the next three prospect meetings I should have been in the room for. The ones after that, I got invited to and didn't win, and I'll never know for certain how much of that was the energy call following me and how much was something else. That uncertainty is its own particular kind of professional haunting. You can't defend yourself against a reputation you can't see.

I ran the numbers later, when enough time had passed that I could look at them without flinching. The energy call, directly, cost me one client and about $340,000 in assets under management. The referrals that didn't happen because of it—the prospects who heard some version of the story before I ever got in the room—probably cost me three times that. Maybe more. I'll never know the actual number, which means I'll never know the full price I paid for letting eighteen months of recent data substitute for the longer record I could have pulled.

Or take Sarah, the engineer who didn't get promoted. She didn't just leave. She left and took institutional knowledge with her—three years of context on the codebase, relationships with the infrastructure team, the specific debugging intuition you only build by living inside a system for that long. The company had to backfill her role. The hiring process took four months. The replacement ramped slowly. The two features Sarah had been scoped to lead in Q1 slipped to Q2, then Q3. One of them got cancelled. The junior developers she'd been mentoring struggled without her. One of them left six months later, citing lack of growth opportunities, which was code for "the person who was teaching me is gone."

The manager didn't intend to be unfair. He just didn't pull the full record. He reconstructed the year from memory in December, and memory gave him November and December in high resolution and January through October in fading detail. Sarah's contributions from the first three quarters weren't erased—they just weren't weighted proportionally. The manager's sense of her year was an average of unequal parts: the recent months counted more because they were easier to retrieve.

Or take the jury. The civil trial ended in a defense verdict. The plaintiff's structural engineer had documented twelve separate code violations, each one photographed and cross-referenced to the building code in writing. The defense contractor cried on the stand and said she'd done her best. The jury believed her. Maybe they were right—I wasn't there, and I didn't see the evidence. But the plaintiff's attorney filed a post-trial motion arguing the verdict was against the weight of the evidence, and two of the jurors later said, in depositions, that they didn't remember the engineer's testimony in detail during deliberations. They remembered he'd testified. They remembered it was technical. But the specifics had faded. The contractor's testimony hadn't faded. It was recent and emotional and vivid, and it was what filled the room when they had to decide.

The cost isn't always dramatic. Sometimes it's cumulative and quiet.

The baseball front office that consistently overvalues players coming off career years and undervalues players whose longer averages predict future performance more accurately pays more for the same production, year after year, until the salary structure stops working and the competitive window closes. That's not one bad contract. That's a systematic pattern that compounds across every negotiation, every arbitration hearing, every trade deadline, every free agency period.

The forecaster who keeps reacting to the most recent data release—extrapolating from it, building conviction from it, letting it dominate the longer trend it's sitting inside—builds a track record that doesn't justify the confidence clients are paying for. Some of the extrapolations turn out right. Some turn out wrong. The batting average hovers around chance. Eventually the clients notice, or they don't notice but they leave anyway because someone else is offering the same coin-flip forecasting at a lower fee.

The couple who lets the memory of the relationship's final, worst months overwrite the fuller history that preceded them makes the wrong call about whether the relationship is fixable. Maybe it wasn't fixable—I'm not arguing every relationship that ends badly should have been saved. But they didn't actually evaluate the full evidence. They evaluated the portion of the evidence memory made easy to retrieve, and memory made the ending easy to retrieve because the ending was recent and emotionally intense. The two years before the ending, when things were mostly fine, faded. Not because those two years didn't matter. Because they weren't recent.

I can hear the objection forming. If the recent evidence is misleading, wouldn't that be obvious while you're looking at it?

No. That's the whole problem.

Recent evidence doesn't feel like a biased sample while you're inside it. It feels like the truth finally clarifying after a period of ambiguity. Eighteen months of rising energy prices didn't feel to me, in December 2014, like noise I should discount. It felt like the signal I'd been waiting for. The structural shift everyone had been talking about for years, finally showing up in the data. I wasn't ignoring the longer history because I was lazy or careless. I was ignoring it because the recent history felt more real.

And here's the worse part: when a roomful of smart, experienced people all have access to the same recent, vivid evidence—and none of them have pulled the full record to compare it against—their shared conviction doesn't average out to an unbiased group judgment. It amplifies. Everyone's recency-weighted impression reinforces everyone else's. The consensus feels earned, careful, deliberative. It's none of those things. It's just several identically distorted individual memories mistaken for independent confirmation.

That's what happened across the energy analyst community in late 2014. We all saw the same eighteen-month run. We all formed the same conviction. We all reinforced each other's certainty. And we were all wrong in the same direction at the same time, not because we were individually foolish but because we were all running the same biased retrieval process and treating the resulting agreement as validation.

The structural answer isn't willpower. It's process. Four techniques recur across the domains this book has examined, and none of them requires unusual discipline once they're actually in place. What they require—every one of them—is being built into the workflow before the vivid, recent evidence shows up, because by the time that evidence is sitting in front of you, competing against an abstract fuller record that's harder to retrieve, the recent evidence has already won.

The first is what I'll call the full-window checklist, though that makes it sound more formal than it needs to be.

The idea is this: before making a consequential judgment, pull the complete relevant record. Don't trust memory. Don't trust the headline. Don't assume the recent period is representative. Actually retrieve the full history and look at it.

The investor evaluating two fund managers doesn't have to rely on last year's return, which is what the marketing materials will emphasize and what will stick most easily in memory. The full ten-year record exists. It's downloadable. The full-window checklist is just the discipline to download it and look at it before making the allocation decision, not after.

I didn't do this in December 2014, and I could have. I had a Bloomberg terminal. I had access to decades of energy sector data. Commodity price cycles were visible if you pulled the window back far enough. I didn't pull it back. I looked at the recent eighteen months, built a story that made those eighteen months feel like the start of something new rather than a short stretch inside a longer mean-reverting cycle, and walked into the meeting confident.

The corrective information existed. I just didn't retrieve it, because the recent information was vivid enough that retrieving anything else felt unnecessary.

The baseball front office that built a formal valuation model weighting career performance over recent seasons is doing the same thing at organizational scale. They've made pulling the full record a required step, not something left to whoever in the room happens to remember to do it. The model forces the question: what does this player's full career baseline predict about future performance, and how much should we adjust that baseline based on last year's outlier?

Sometimes the answer is "adjust a lot"—the outlier year was the player finally healthy, or finally getting plate discipline, or finally figuring out how to hit the breaking ball. Sometimes the answer is "don't adjust much"—the outlier year was luck, or a contract year, or a small-sample hot streak that regression will erase. The model doesn't make the judgment for you. It just forces you to make the judgment from the full record instead of from the part of the record that's easiest to remember.

This is closely related to base-rate reasoning, which gets covered in more technical depth in other places. But the core insight is narrow and practical. A base rate is just the long-run average outcome across a full relevant population or history. That's exactly the kind of quantity a full-window checklist surfaces. And once you've actually assembled the full history and put it side by side with the recent chapter, the recent chapter stops dominating by default. It still gets weight. It just doesn't get all the weight.

You might think you'd do this naturally. That when the stakes are high and the decision matters, you'd automatically pull the full record before committing.

You wouldn't. I didn't. And I had every incentive to get it right.

The second technique is contemporaneous documentation.

If memory decays unevenly—and it does—then don't rely on memory. Write it down. At the time it happens.

The software company that implemented continuous feedback for performance reviews removed the recency problem from the annual review process entirely. Managers don't reconstruct the employee's year from memory in December. They pull up the written record: the feedback logged in February after the successful feature launch, the note from May about the mentoring work, the observation from August about the production bug Sarah caught. The fuller record exists somewhere other than the manager's fading, recency-weighted memory, which means the December review can actually reflect the full year.

This isn't complicated. It's just a practice: when something worth noting happens, note it. Don't wait until review season and try to reconstruct twelve months of contributions from recall.

The courtroom version is juror note-taking and access to trial transcripts during deliberation. When jurors can consult a written record of the structural engineer's Tuesday testimony, they're not asking memory to hold four days of evidence in equal focus. The written record holds it for them. The contractor's emotional Thursday testimony still registers—recent and vivid information doesn't stop being recent and vivid just because a transcript exists. But the transcript gives the older information a way to compete. Without it, memory does the weighting, and memory weights recent information more heavily than older information of equal or greater relevance.

Some jurisdictions allow this. Some don't. The ones that don't are implicitly betting that twelve people's unaided memories will produce a more accurate collective judgment than twelve people with access to a written record of what was actually said. I don't know how to make that bet sound reasonable.

The relationship version is softer, less formal, but it's the same underlying technique. A periodic check-in—monthly, quarterly, whatever rhythm actually works for the people involved—creates a contemporaneous record of how the relationship is actually going, not a reconstruction from memory six months later when things have gotten hard. The check-in doesn't prevent the relationship from getting hard. It just prevents the hard final months from overwriting the fuller history in memory, because the fuller history exists in writing, dated, from back when it was happening.

I started keeping a version of this after losing Michael Chen.

Nothing elaborate. Just a dated, one-paragraph summary of every significant recommendation I made, written the day I made it, capturing the specific evidence I was relying on at the time. I don't edit it later. I don't try to make past entries look smarter in hindsight. I just write down what I actually believed and why, and then I leave it alone.

When I go back and read those entries months later, the gap between what I actually believed at the time and what I remember believing is—honestly—unnerving. Memory doesn't just fade. It rewrites. I'll remember being more cautious on a call than I actually was, or more confident, depending on how the call turned out. I'll remember considering risks I didn't actually consider, or downplaying risks I actually spent three paragraphs worrying about. The written record doesn't let me get away with that. It shows me what I actually thought, in my own words, before I knew how it would turn out.

It's a small practice. But it directly addresses the failure I couldn't fix through effort alone: the silent substitution of a reconstructed, recency-weighted memory for the thing that actually happened.

The third technique is pre-registering the decision criterion.

Set the standard before the vivid recent evidence arrives.

A pre-mortem, in its most common form, asks a group to imagine a decision has already failed and work backward to identify what could have caused the failure. It's designed to surface risks that in-the-moment urgency and enthusiasm tend to suppress. The version most relevant here is narrower: a valuation model, a trend-filtering rule, or an explicit decision criterion, built and documented before any specific recent data point shows up to argue for an exception.

The baseball front office that requires a written justification to exceed the valuation model's recommended contract offer has made this move. So has the quantitative forecasting methodology that requires an on-the-record case for treating a new data point as signal rather than noise, with the case made explicit before the forecast gets updated.

The discipline is this: a standard set in writing before the vivid evidence showed up is much harder for that evidence to silently bend than a standard being formed for the first time in the same moment the evidence is being weighed.

I didn't have a pre-registered criterion in December 2014. I had a general sense that energy looked attractive, and when eighteen months of strong performance landed in front of me, I let that recent performance become the justification for the overweight position rather than asking whether it met a standard I'd set in advance. If I'd written down, beforehand, what would actually constitute evidence of a durable regime shift in the commodity cycle versus a short-term rally inside a longer mean-reverting pattern, the eighteen-month run wouldn't have been enough. The supply data was already loosening. The demand signals were already shifting. But I didn't have the standard written down beforehand, which meant I formed it in the moment, which meant the vivid recent evidence got to shape the standard itself.

That's the failure mode this technique prevents. You can't bend a rule you wrote last year to fit the exciting new evidence you're looking at today. You can decide the rule was wrong and change it—but you have to do that explicitly, on the record, which creates enough friction that you'll only do it when the case for changing the rule is actually strong.

The fourth technique is assigning the longer-horizon role.

In a group decision, formally designate someone whose explicit job is to argue from the full history against the pull of the most recent information.

This addresses a dynamic that's shown up repeatedly across the earlier chapters: a group of independently recency-biased individuals doesn't average out to an unbiased group judgment. Each person's biased impression reinforces the others'. The resulting consensus feels like careful collective deliberation. It isn't. It's the amplified sum of several identically distorted individual memories mistaken for independent confirmation.

A formally assigned longer-horizon role breaks the loop. Someone in the room has standing—explicit, sanctioned standing—to ask, "What does the full record actually show, not just the most recent chapter?" And because it's their assigned role, they're not paying the social price for looking contrarian or overly cautious. They're just doing their job.

That question is much more likely to get asked, and taken seriously, when asking it is someone's designated role than when it depends on an individual's willingness to volunteer it unprompted.

This is a structural answer to the asymmetric-cost problem that showed up across multiple domains earlier in the book. The sports executive who correctly discounts a player's hot streak pays a social cost if the hot streak continues and the team passed on the player. The forecaster who correctly resists an extrapolative consensus pays a career cost if the trend continues and their caution looks like timidity. The campaign staffer who correctly dismisses a dramatic but ultimately noisy news cycle pays a status cost if the news cycle actually moves polling and the campaign looks flat-footed for not responding.

Assigning the longer-horizon argument as a formal role, rather than hoping someone will volunteer it, lowers the personal cost of making the case. You're not being contrarian. You're doing what you were asked to do.

Bridgewater Associates, the hedge fund, institutionalized a version of this in their decision-making process. They don't just encourage dissent. They assign it. In major investment decisions, someone is formally tasked with making the bear case, and someone else is formally tasked with making the bull case, and both cases get argued and documented before the decision gets made. The assigned bear isn't pessimistic by nature. The assigned bull isn't optimistic by nature. They're just playing roles that force the full range of evidence—including the less recent, less vivid evidence—into the room.

Does any of this actually work, or does it just sound reasonable in theory?

There's independent support, and it comes from research that wasn't designed with recency bias in mind.

Philip Tetlock ran a multi-year study tracking thousands of people making predictions on real geopolitical questions—Would Greece exit the eurozone? Would oil hit $200 a barrel? Would North Korea's regime collapse?—and scored every prediction against its eventual outcome. The research compared the habits of the most accurate forecasters, the ones who came to be called superforecasters, against everyone else.

The specific habits that separated the strongest performers weren't exotic. They were structural, and they were learnable.

The best forecasters updated their views incrementally as new evidence arrived. They didn't swing their probability estimates wildly on every fresh headline. When a new data point came in, they adjusted—but the adjustment was proportionate to the weight of the new information relative to everything they already knew. They didn't let the newest piece of evidence dominate just because it was newest.

They kept explicit, revisitable records of their own past predictions and reasoning, rather than relying on memory to reconstruct what they'd believed and when. That let them learn from their mistakes honestly, without the memory distortions that make every past forecast look more cautious or more prescient than it actually was at the time.

And they treated any single new data point as one update among many, not as grounds for wholesale revision of their view. A new poll, a new economic release, a new statement from a foreign leader—it all got weighted, but it didn't get to override the full base of evidence the forecast was sitting on.

Those habits map almost exactly onto the four techniques this chapter just described: pulling the full record, documenting judgments contemporaneously, setting standards in advance, and building in a longer-horizon check against the pull of recent information.

Tetlock's research wasn't studying recency bias specifically. It was studying forecasting accuracy generally. But the habits it identified as distinguishing skilled forecasters from unskilled ones converge, with unusual precision, on the same small set of correctives this book has been circling. That's its own form of confirmation. Different research traditions, studying different populations, answering different questions, landing on the same techniques.

And Tetlock's account is explicit that these habits are learnable. They improve with deliberate practice. Forecasting accuracy isn't a fixed trait. It's a skill that responds to training, and the training that works is procedural, not motivational. You don't get better at forecasting by trying harder or caring more. You get better by adopting specific structural habits that correct for the specific, predictable ways human judgment fails.

That's a modestly encouraging finding for a book that has spent eight chapters documenting how automatic and resistant to willpower this bias is. Automatic doesn't mean permanently fixed. It just means the correction has to come in the form of a structured, practiced habit, not a one-time resolution to be more careful.

Adopting any of these techniques inside a real organization, though, runs into a specific and predictable obstacle.

The person proposing a full-window checklist, or a pre-registered decision criterion, or a formally assigned devil's advocate is—in the short run—proposing to slow down a decision everyone else in the room feels ready to make. And if the decision would have been right without the extra step, the extra step looks like unnecessary caution afterward. Not prudent discipline. Caution.

This is the same asymmetric-cost problem the earlier chapters kept encountering. The techniques are cheap to describe and expensive to adopt, because adopting them means accepting, in advance, that some fraction of the friction they introduce will turn out to have been unnecessary in hindsight.

Organizations that successfully build these techniques into practice tend to share one feature: they treat the cost as known and budgeted, not as a failure.

A full-window checklist that occasionally slows down a decision that would have been correct anyway isn't malfunctioning. It's functioning as designed. The same way a smoke detector that occasionally goes off because of burnt toast is functioning as designed. You're not trying to eliminate false positives. You're trying to catch the true positives—the decisions that would have been wrong without the extra check—at a tolerable rate of false alarms.

The tolerance is the hard part. It requires someone senior enough to enforce it to actually believe the technique is worth the friction. If the person at the top of the decision chain doesn't believe it, the technique dies the first time it slows down a decision that turns out to have been right, because someone in the room will say, "See? We didn't need the extra step. We should just move faster next time."

I've seen this happen. A team adopts a pre-mortem process. The first three decisions they run through it, the pre-mortem surfaces a real risk they hadn't considered, and they adjust, and the decisions turn out better for it. The fourth decision, the pre-mortem doesn't surface anything new. The decision would have been fine without it. Someone says, "We spent an hour on this and didn't get anything out of it. Maybe we don't need to do this every time." The process dies quietly over the next two months, and six months later they make a decision that blows up in exactly the way a pre-mortem would have caught.

The corrective is remembering that the goal isn't perfection. It's improving the base rate. If the technique catches three bad decisions and adds friction to seven harmless ones, it's working. You just have to be willing to pay the cost of the seven to catch the three.

If you're not working inside an organization with formal review processes or procedural safeguards—if you're just trying to make your own decisions less vulnerable to this—the personal version is simpler.

Keep a written, dated record of significant judgments and predictions. Not everything. Just the ones that matter. Make the record at the time you form the judgment, not later. Write down what you believe and why, in enough detail that you'll be able to tell, six months from now, what evidence you were actually relying on.

Then revisit it. Not obsessively. Just periodically. Once a quarter is probably enough.

The revisiting does two things. First, it shows you how your memory has rewritten your past beliefs, which is uncomfortable but useful. You'll see yourself remembering more caution than you actually felt, or more confidence, depending on how things turned out. That's the recency effect running in reverse—your memory of your past judgment getting distorted by your knowledge of the outcome.

Second, it lets you learn from your mistakes honestly. If you predicted something would happen and it didn't, you can go back and see what you were thinking at the time, what evidence you weighted heavily, what you missed. That's actual learning. It's much harder to do that from unaided memory, because memory has already started rewriting the narrative to make you look better.

I keep my record in a simple text file. One entry per decision. Date, what I recommended, what evidence I was relying on, what I expected to happen. I don't dress it up. I just write it down and leave it.

It's the smallest of the four techniques, and it's the one I actually use consistently, because it doesn't require anyone else's buy-in and it doesn't slow down any process I'm part of. It just requires me to spend three minutes writing something down after I've made a judgment that matters.

Three minutes. That's the cost.

The benefit is that six months later, when I'm trying to figure out whether I actually learned anything from the judgment or whether I just got lucky or unlucky, I have something to work with besides my own unreliable reconstruction.

I still make mistakes. I still let recent evidence dominate sometimes when it shouldn't. But I make fewer mistakes than I did in

December 2014, and when I do make them, I can see them clearly enough afterward to have a chance of not making the same one twice.

That's not perfection. It's just a slightly better base rate, compounded over enough decisions that it matters.

The energy call cost me Michael Chen and however many referrals I'll never know about. I can't get those back. What I can do is make sure the next time I'm sitting across from someone with a thesis that feels compelling because recent performance is running in its favor, I pull the full record before I walk into the room. Not because I'll always get the call right. Because I'll get it wrong less often, and for better reasons, and I'll know the difference.

Also in the Series

Every book in The Bias Files stands on its own — read them in any order. If this one was useful, the library continues:

Blind Trust

Can't Let Go

The Planted Price

Why We Fear the Wrong Things

The Expert Trap

Blinded by Brilliance

Cutting Losses

I Knew It All Along

Why Smart People Do Stupid Things

When Everyone's Buying, Sell

The Invisible Failures

Why Bad Beats Good

Why It's Never Your Fault

Twice as Long

Words Are Weapons

When Everyone Agrees, You're Wrong

It's Not Them, It's You

www.ingramcontent.com/pod-product-compliance
Lightning Source LLC
LaVergne TN
LVHW010722061126
851857LV00014B/1305

* 9 7 8 1 8 0 4 2 8 2 0 5 2 *